ACTING IN FAITH

ACTING IN FAITH

The World Council of Churches since 1975

Leon Howell

World Council of Churches, Geneva

Cover and illustrations: Paul Peter Piech
ISBN No. 2-8254-0708-9
© 1982 World Council of Churches, 150, route de Ferney,
1211 Geneva 20, Switzerland
Printed in Switzerland

TABLE OF CONTENTS

INTRODUCTION

Above all else, the World Council of Churches is an expression of faith. Its 301 member churches from almost a hundred countries differ markedly. They come from a wide variety of confessional traditions, worship in hundreds of languages, live under a jumble of political orders, emerge from contrasting historical experiences, express their hope in vastly different cultures.

But they have joined together in a world council of churches because of their common faith. "Now faith is the assurance of things hoped for, the conviction of things not seen" (Heb. 11:1).

The basis

Together they affirm that the World Council is a "fellowship of churches which confess the Lord Jesus Christ as God and Saviour according to the scriptures and therefore seek to fulfill their common calling to the glory of one God, Father, Son and Holy Spirit".

The vast majority of Reformation, Orthodox and Anglican churches has come to affirm this "basis" (as it is called in the constitution) as a sign of their willingness to journey together on an ecumenical adventure.

Through their common instrument, the World Council of Churches (WCC), these 301 churches represent almost 400 million Christians.

The "basis" is not a full confession of faith. Membership is open to any church that accepts the "basis"; by it the Council defines its nature and clarifies membership limits. (Clearly limits are there; no secular organization, no political party, no religious body other than Christian could belong.)

The commitment is moral; how seriously membership is taken is not a matter which can be legislated. "Any authority the Council will have will consist in the weight which it carries with the churches by its own wisdom," said ecumenical pioneer William Temple.

Thus the Council is not a universal authority which controls what Christians should believe or prescribes what they should do. "The

1

World Council is an entirely novel attempt at the churches being in concert together," General Secretary Philip Potter has said.

The faith the churches have in common is more clear to those who have experienced it than to those who have not. Theologian Robert McAfee Brown attended the 1975 Assembly in Nairobi, Kenya. Afterwards he wrote:

> Despite differences of ecclesiastical tradition, economic fortune and linguistic background, the delegates were united by a commonly shared faith, a faith in Jesus Christ who — in a mysterious way not completely clear even after 19 days of pursuing the theme — both *frees* and *unites*.*
>
> That difference makes all the difference. What drew people to the assembly, and what sustained them during some hectic, tense and occasionally boring sessions, was a faith that somehow Jesus Christ makes a difference, a crucial difference, and that it was worth all the pain and tension and cost and insecurity to keep exploring that liberating and uniting fact.

The history

That act of faith, that acting in faith, which created the WCC in 1948, was the culmination of a process that had its most obvious roots in the early years of the twentieth century.

The Christian church, through the remarkable chapter of its history known as the missionary movement, had helped to plant the church in all parts of the world. It had broken out of its Western parochialism. But the scandal of its disunity was increasingly felt in Asia and Africa, challenging the consciences of a growing number of Christians.

As Ans van der Bent, librarian of the Ecumenical Centre in Geneva, has written (in *What in the World is the World Council of Churches?*):

> When Martin Luther pinned his Ninety-five Theses to the door of the chapel of Wittenberg Castle in 1517, he had no idea that the solid stem of the church he challenged would soon be split into a thousand branches. Reforming the church in Geneva, John Calvin was unable to see the schism ahead between the Church of England and Rome in 1570. Still less could he foresee the formation of Congregational, Baptist and Methodist churches in Great Britain, let alone Mennonite, Brethren, Disciples of Christ, Old Catholic Churches in Europe and North America.

---

* The theme of the Nairobi Assembly was *Jesus Christ Frees and Unites*.

But the division in the church had begun long before Luther. Five centuries before the Reformation a great schism between Greek and Latin churches had already taken place. From 1054 onward Eastern churches continued to celebrate the divine liturgy according to the Byzantine rite and rejected the authority of the Pope in Rome. Orthodoxy became a self-contained world of its own and almost nine hundred years were to pass before Western theologians began to take serious notice of Orthodox theology. Only after World War II did churches in the West start to care about the life of millions of Orthodox Christians in the socialist countries.

In fact, church concern of any sort that crossed denominational lines was in short supply. Until the beginning of this century, nearly all Christian churches lived in self-centred isolation. Each church, small or large, pointed to its own tradition, celebrated its own liturgy, shepherded the needs of its own flock and was preoccupied with its own identity. The idea of churches together rendering witness and service to the world was foreign. Theology was carried on in the form of confessional monologues.

The modern ecumenical movement ("ecumenical" is from the Greek word, *oikoumene*, the whole inhabited world) is most commonly traced to the World Mission Conference in Edinburgh in 1910. Mission agencies of the churches met to plan mission strategy — "the evangelization of the world in our generation" was a slogan used by John R. Mott, one of the organizers of this meeting — and a more coordinated approach to mission.

Shortly after World War I had shattered some of the presumptions of Western Christendom, 1920 brought three very special meetings to Switzerland. One followed up the Edinburgh meeting and planned the creation of the International Missionary Council (IMC) which emerged formally in 1921. A second brought together those anxious to tackle the difficult issues of doctrine which separated the churches. From this came the Faith and Order movement which had its first world meeting in Lausanne in 1927. The third set in motion "Life and Work" which was born officially in Stockholm in 1925 as the Universal Conference of the Church of Christ on Life and Work. Identified with the phrase, "Service unites; doctrine divides", Life and Work wanted to relate the Christian faith to international relations and to social, industrial and economic life.

Dr Willem A. Visser 't Hooft, first General Secretary of the WCC, recalls that at that time "it seemed that these organizations were so different that it would be impossible to bring them together. Cooperation in missions; unity in doctrine and church order; common action in society — these seemed to require different

3

approaches. But there were a few men of vision and imagination who looked ahead towards a more inclusive goal."

Their vision prevailed. By 1938 Faith and Order (F&O) and Life and Work (L&W) had in fact been led to establish a World Council of Churches. But World War II intervened. Visser 't Hooft was called to staff the World Council of Churches (in process of formation). Working almost alone from Geneva, he helped the churches to support work among prisoners of war, chaplaincy services, preparation for Christian aid in reconstruction after the war, refugee work, and to maintain some ties with the Evangelical Church in Germany.

The World Council of Churches finally arrived with its first assembly in Amsterdam in 1948. Saying "we intend to stay together", it was established by 146 predominantly Western churches (only 30 came from Africa, Asia, and Latin America).

What was taking place through the years and took full shape in 1948 was a decision that the independent ecumenical streams — mission movements and life and work, youth and Bible societies — would now flow into an organization of the churches. It was a crucial decision, one debated even today when those involved in ecumenical action from below or outside the churches wonder if the churches indeed were the right, even a possible, vehicle of unity.

Visser 't Hooft believes that while ecumenical momentum still comes in essential ways from outside the church institutions, the ecumenical movement cannot be "healthy... *without* the churches.... This is the only way to give the ecumenical movement substance in history. An ecumenical movement which is completely non-institutional or even anti-institutional can produce firm ideas of unity, but cannot produce concrete results."

He warns that a defeatism which sees the churches incapable of renewal is as false as the triumphalism which claims for them now what can only be claimed for the church triumphant at the end of time. "As men and women of the ecumenical movement, we have special reason to speak with gratitude about the churches. They have to a considerable extent responded to the call to come out of their isolation, to enter into dialogue, to assist each other, to take common action in meeting human need, to speak out together against oppression and injustice."

The result

They came out. They decided to stay together. They have stayed together. And others have joined. Today churches from all continents and all worlds — first, second and third — are involved in this expression of faith. A handful of churches have left — often receiving considerable publicity — but many have come in, and keep coming in — without receiving any publicity.

If the WCC is a "privileged instrument" of the ecumenical movement, it is not itself the ecumenical movement. Most important is the way the barriers have crumbled among people all around the world, who work, pray, confess, struggle and live their faith together. For many, the structural roadblocks still in the way of the "visible unity" the WCC seeks are of little consequence. Where it counts, we are already one. General Secretary Philip Potter described these signs of the new community to the Central Committee of the WCC in these words:

All over the world there are Christian communities which are signs of life and joy. There are those who dare to challenge the forces of death and of despair with the message of the kingdom of God and his justice. These base communities; these people's movements; these lay centres; these small experiments in participation in development through self-reliance; these groups working for community health care and seeking to be healing communities; these worshipping congregations creating new songs and liturgies and supporting one another in a solidarity of faith and witness; these persons who risk or suffer imprisonment, torture and death for their joyful testimony to God's just rule; these simple, conservative believers who allow their eyes to be opened to the world around them and take the first tentative steps to reach out to their fellow human beings in need — these are all manifestations of the community of life and joy, of the communion of the saints.

From this rich experience comes the continuing momentum for the ecumenical movement. The Roman Catholic Church, with over 600 million members, also works for the unity of all Christians. Its attitude has changed radically since Pope John XXIII called the Second Vatican Council twenty years ago. That Council's Decree on Ecumenism praised "the ecumenical sincerity and energy of the separated brethren".

Pope John XXIII created in 1960 a Secretariat for the Promotion of Christian Unity to coordinate all ecumenical relations with other churches. Since 1965 annual meetings have taken place in the Joint Working Group, with members appointed by the Vatican and the WCC, to discuss common issues among their members.

Pope Paul VI visited the WCC in 1969 and called the occasion "a prophetic moment and truly blessed encounter". Pope John Paul II also intends to visit; earlier plans made for 1981 had to be cancelled because of the attempt on his life.

The Roman Catholic Church has become a full member of more than twenty national councils of churches as well as the Caribbean and Pacific regional councils. A number of Roman Catholics are full members of the Faith and Order Commission. Eventual membership in the WCC by the Roman Catholic Church, with all the complexities that suggests, is still an open question.

National councils exist in many nations. So do regional councils; the Christian Conference of Asia is the oldest; 1982 will see a constituent assembly for the Latin American Council of Churches, already in process of formation.

Add to that 12 international confessional organs, of which the Lutheran World Federation, the World Alliance of Reformed Churches, and the World Methodist Council have their offices with the WCC in the Ecumenical Centre in Geneva. So also do the Conference of European Churches, and representatives of the Russian Orthodox Church and the Ecumenical Patriarchate in Constantinople.

Establishing and maintaining relationships "with national councils and regional councils of churches, world confessional bodies, and other ecumenical organizations" is another constitutional "function" of the WCC.

The work

A warning before describing in summary how the WCC operates. It is not possible to write about the Council without referring endlessly to cities where crucial meetings occurred and decisions were made. That is already evident in this brief introduction. Margaret Mead, the great anthropologist, attended her first WCC meeting in 1962, a committee discussing racism. "I tried to feel my way through the maze of cities around which so much history clustered," she wrote in *Christianity and Crisis* magazine. "Every time someone said, 'But that was at Amsterdam' (1948), or 'But after Evanston' (1954), I got Daisuke Kitagawa (then on the WCC staff), whom I was sitting next to, to write down the date."

In a beginner's guide to ecumenical English, *One World,* the WCC's "popular" monthly magazine, offered, tongue-in-cheek, this definition, among others: "What was proposed at Bossey, agreed on at Nairobi, implemented in Berlin, is now being evaluated at Bombay." Which is to be interpreted: "...the significance of any ecumenical decision is measured by adding the distance between the meetings it involved".

6

The plan is to write this book in a way that people not saturated in WCC history and experience can read it. After all, if anthropologist Margaret Mead got confused..... That is the intention. But, alas, cities are benchmarks in this endeavour and cities will be mentioned.

Such as Amsterdam, Evanston, New Delhi, Uppsala, Nairobi, and Vancouver. The supreme legislative body governing the World Council, proclaims the constitution, is the Assembly which shall ordinarily meet at seven-year intervals. It is composed of official delegates of member churches which elect those delegates. Which says nothing of the richness and complexity of a gathering of so many people from so many cultures and traditions speaking hundreds of languages. The assemblies, beyond their constitutional status, have been the places where the churches read the "signs of the time" and where the Council and the churches have expressed their mutual accountability. They have been the primary focus of the Council's work.

It all began in Amsterdam (1948). The Second Assembly gathered in the midst of Cold War tensions in Evanston (near Chicago, USA). Held in New Delhi, India, in 1961, the Third Assembly is remembered as the first outside the West, because the International Missionary Council (IMC) was integrated into the WCC, and because the Orthodox churches in the socialist countries joined. Uppsala (near Stockholm, Sweden) was the site of the Fourth Assembly in 1968. This assembly confronted the churches with the challenges of the 1960s: racism, the growing gap between poor and rich nations, the student revolts, and the ambiguity of new scientific and technological "progress". Nairobi, Kenya, was the site of the Fifth Assembly. By this time the meeting, which involved almost 3,000 delegates, consultants, visitors and press, had grown into a complex event requiring years of preparation. The churches now move towards their Sixth Assembly in Vancouver, Canada, in July-August 1983. The theme will be *Jesus Christ — the Life of the World.*

Archbishop Edward Scott of Canada said in 1980 that he believed "viewing an assembly held every seven years as the main point for focusing the main accountability between the Council and the member churches is outmoded". The Council is too large, its activities too varied, and events move too swiftly. That would suggest a continuing process of interaction and dialogue "between the Council and its member churches which has a number of focal points, of which the assembly is a very important one but not the only one".

Scott, Primate of the Anglican Church in Canada, is Moderator of the Central Committee of the WCC. The Committee, which currently has 134 members, is elected by the assembly to meet annually to act on its behalf between assemblies. Scott also chairs a much smaller Executive Committee which meets more often. From the Central Committee comes the nomination of individuals to commissions and working groups overseeing the work of the staff. Altogether in 1981 some 250 men and 75 women from a large cross-section of the membership of the WCC were regularly involved in planning and overseeing the Council's programmes and activities.

Scott was speaking to the 1980 Central Committee meeting which decided that visits between and among member churches and regional councils should be a priority for 1982 and up to the Vancouver assembly. Staff would be involved, as would standing committees. This would broaden the scope of the assembly, allow for communication between the churches and the Council, and involve delegates long before Vancouver. (Eighty per cent of the Nairobi delegates had never been to an assembly before. That was good in many ways, but it also required valuable time for delegates to be introduced to the intricacies of an assembly.)

This book is essentially about the work of the WCC since the Nairobi assembly. It is in no sense an official account of all its work. It is completed in early 1982 when the WCC staff will be devoting much of their time to assembly planning and the visits. The world does not stop and the Council will not either. But major conferences and consultations will not now be held before the assembly. The Nairobi period is close to completion.

The offices of the WCC where daily work is carried on are located in the Ecumenical Centre in Geneva in a four-storey building just above the UN and near the World Health Organization (WHO) and International Labour Office (ILO) buildings. The staff is made up of 280 people (October 1981) from all over the world, of whom 110 are executive or programme staff.

One of the complaints about the WCC is that its staff is too large, that it is too bureaucratic. Perhaps. Neighbours ILO and WHO, for example, respectively have in Geneva 1,374 and 1,100 employees. One large Christian lay academy in the Federal Republic of Germany has a staff of almost 200. Administering an international organization is a complex task. Eight of the WCC's staff are translators, who try in at least a few languages to make the WCC's documents and meetings accessible. To answer whether there are too many staff requires first asking what is expected. A short answer, based on my limited observation, would be that, given what the churches ask of the staff, it is at least as arguable that the Council is understaffed as overstaffed.

8

Since 1971 the tasks in Geneva have been divided into three primary units, each of which has four or five sub-units. Unit I is Faith and Witness (sub-units: Church and Society, Dialogue with People of Living Faiths and Ideologies, Faith and Order, World Mission and Evangelism). Unit II is Justice and Service (sub-units: Interchurch Aid, Refugee and World Service, International Affairs, Churches' Commission for Participation in Development, Programme to Combat Racism, Christian Medical Commission). Unit III is Education and Renewal (sub-units: Education, Progamme on Theological Education, Renewal and Congregational Life, Women in Church and Society, Youth).

More will be said later about the work of the individual sub-units. The purpose of the unit arrangement is to seek closer working relationships within the units and the Council. Each unit has a staff moderator who also serves the General Secretariat as a Deputy General Secretary. Prof. Todor Sabev (Bulgaria) is moderator for Faith and Witness, Dr Konrad Raiser (Federal Republic of Germany) for Justice and Service, and Mrs Marie Assaad (Egypt) for Education and Renewal.

The tensions

In spite of serious intentions to work together, the various parts of the Council do run into organizational problems. The Nairobi Assembly emphasized the need for the Council to be seen as a whole. "Spiritual, prophetic and enabling dimensions are inseparable for the total life and work of the WCC as it acts both with the member churches and for the member churches."

As he left the WCC staff in 1978 after eight years, the Rev. Alan Brash told *One World* that the structure of the WCC currently is "bedevilled by its history". The WCC is a federation

of bodies who agreed to unite but didn't truly marry, and they've kept their own separateness as well as their unity, not in budgeting but in concept, constituency and so on. And while some of that is necessary, that's what I would fight — the separateness of it all.

The bad structures in the World Council, apart from our own inefficiencies, are mostly the creation of the churches. They insist on earmarking and channelling all their money in very strict organizational terms. They not only say: "We want this to go to the Sahel disaster," they also say: "We want this to be administered by that unit and nobody else." To my mind, this disintegrates the real authority of the Council.

The lack of interaction between questions of unity, evangelism, education, renewal, service, and the quest for justice and peace has seriously harmed the churches. "Churches have tended to emphasize one major aspect or another of our Christian calling according to their historic calling," Philip Potter has said.

It has led to a division of concerns within the churches which has seriously affected Christians. This is especially true "of the churches' prophetic witness on social and political issues", according to Potter. "The training of Christians in faith has been truncated and so they have not been able to connect their faith with their actions in the world. Nor have they been able to discern the consequences of their actions for their understanding of their faith and their life together."

The special task of the General Secretariat of the WCC — the General Secretary and three Deputy General Secretaries, the Communication Department, the Finance Department, the Library of the Ecumenical Centre, the New York Office, and the Ecumenical Institute at nearby Bossey — is to see the whole in the many parts, and to help the units and the churches do the same.

More than one person, sensing my confusion as I encountered the separateness of the WCC efforts within the also evident concern for unified work, told me to read Philip Potter's addresses to the Central Committee (reprinted after every meeting in *The Ecumenical Review*), his speeches and sermons, and the book, *Life in all its Fullness* (published in 1981, incorporating many of his addresses and speeches), and, of course, to talk with him.

Dr Potter became General Secretary of the WCC at the end of 1972, after previously serving the WCC as Director of the Commission on World Mission and Evangelism (CWME) and, much earlier, as Director of the Youth Department. He is the third General Secretary — Dr Visser 't Hooft and Dr Eugene Carson Blake preceded him — and the first third world person to hold the position.

The ecumenical movement has provided considerable opportunity for the "universal dialogue of cultures" to which Potter often refers. In this exchange people and churches are challenged to understand the fullness of God's revelation and to overcome their own parochialism. This has often been a liberating and changing experience. It can also be painful. Alan Brash, of the Presbyterian Church in New Zealand, has written that no church is entirely comfortable in the WCC, nor should it expect to be. Living and working with people who are not like us, Brash says, in doctrine, worship, life-style, cultural background, language, political persuasion, "is always uncomfortable". An Orthodox writer referred to it as a "permanent tension".

10

What they meant was well illustrated at the CWME World Mission Conference in Melbourne in 1980 (the meeting is in a direct line from Edinburgh, 1910) by Orthodox Metropolitan Geevarghese Mar Osthathios from Kerala, India. We all have our partial gospel, he said. It is either

> in the form of a Christ-monism, with no role for the Holy Spirit, or the charismatic gospel with no social concerns, or the Unitarian gospel with hardly anything more than what our Jewish or Islamic friends preach. The Roman Catholic Church has its infallible pope, the Protestant brethren the infallible Bible, the Orthodox the infallible Tradition with a capital "T" and hardly anyone has the full implication of the trinitarian faith with the equality it demands.

Recognizing our partial faith is never easy, Alan Brash says that at times the strain becomes too much and the possibility of leaving the WCC is seriously debated. But that has rarely happened, which he finds significant. The challenge and experience of being members are recognized as closely linked "to their ultimate task and reason for existence. To leave the WCC would not just be a withdrawal from a very imperfect organization; it would be in some way a betrayal of a part of their Christian calling."

The tension is inherent in the way the Council has been conceived. Among its functions and purposes are to "call the churches to the goal of visible unity", to facilitate "the common witness of the churches", to "support the churches in their worldwide missionary and evangelistic task", to "express the common concern of the churches in the service of human need, the breaking down of barriers between people, and the promotion of one human family in justice and peace", and to "foster the renewal of the churches in unity, worship, mission and service".

These imply both a service — to be a meeting place for the diversity of the Christian churches — and a prophetic role. The Council, to repeat, is not a super-church; when it speaks, it is to the churches and not for them. No church is bound by what it says. But since it speaks and acts as an agent of the churches, no individual church can completely ignore it and be true to itself. While obeying its mandate, bringing together all aspects of the ecumenical movement, the Council has promoted, according to Potter, "an integrated approach as an expression of the true marks of the life and witness of the church". This role has been affirmed, not without debate or resistance, by the member churches. Thus, the Council has acted unceasingly "to open up the consciousness of the church to the world God loves".

11

In 1980, the last witness to the ecumenical pioneers, Dr Visser 't Hooft, celebrated his 80th birthday. He retired as WCC General Secretary in 1966 but maintains an office at the Ecumenical Centre as a lifetime honorary president. His remarks at an event honouring him on his birthday make important reading (*The Ecumenical Review,* October 1980). He got close to the ecumenical consensus when he observed that in 1968 at the Uppsala Assembly he had said: "It must become clear that church members who deny in fact their responsibility for the needy in any part of the world are just as much guilty of heresy as those who deny this or that article of faith." To his surprise these words, which seemed to him a biblical truth long affirmed by the ecumenical movement, were more widely quoted than anything he had ever said. The "echo" was so sharp that he wondered if he had been misunderstood. So a few years later he said: "Church members who deny that God has reconciled men and women to himself in Christ are just as guilty of heresy as those who refuse to be involved in the struggle for justice and freedom in the world and who do nothing to help their fellow human beings in need."

The gains
In this ecumenical arena, then, the give and take goes on. And, remarkably, this acting in faith has produced a considerably richer understanding of what the full content of that faith is. The fact is that many problems remain, that the visible unity sought has come much more slowly than prayed for, that not enough of the ecumenical experience has penetrated to local parishes and congregations, that the early excitement and expectation have given way to weariness and near despair.

But it is also necessary to understand how far faith has brought the churches. When the Council was formed in 1948, it was world in name only: many third world churches were still dependent, few Orthodox were members. Today the WCC includes churches from all over the world, free to make their contribution to the dialogue of cultures. A number of Pentecostal churches have joined the Orthodox, Anglican and Protestant traditions within the WCC. The Roman Catholic Church is now very much a part of the ecumenical movement. The movement involves the widest range of colours and women are no longer in the background. In various ways the churches talk to each other, challenge each other, learn from each other, and witness together.

Given the centuries of hostility, mistrust, and fear of one another, this has been "no mean achievement in so short a time", Philip

Potter has said. It is too often taken for granted. "We do not often enough rejoice and give thanks that God has drawn his people together in this miraculous way, using such instruments as the World Council of Churches."

* * *

Six years have passed since the Nairobi Assembly. For the WCC they have been filled with signs of great hope and events that brought sighs too deep for words. A financial crisis deepened, crimping WCC involvements. But that crisis was the result of foreign exchange fluctuations in a troubled world economy, not of slackened support from the churches. Some sense a new insularity in the churches, a weariness that inhibits the ecumenical process. But theological agreements on difficult doctrinal issues offer a new possibility for "conciliar unity". Suffering in many places is acute and overwhelming, and respect for human rights appears, in spite of all we say and do, declining. But there are instances where the people speak, and the involvement of the poor in demanding justice and testifying to their faith provides new energy for the Council. Talk of "limited deployment" introduces a new and terrifying uncertainty to the balance of nuclear terror. But mass movements rise up to challenge the assumptions. The Salvation Army withdraws its membership, to a blast of publicity, and, in media silence, three black churches from Southern Africa join the Council at the same time. Racism, sexism and class still divide the church and the human community. But women and men around the world discuss the potential for community when both are full participants. The WCC undergoes the most vicious political attacks in its history but the end to the slaughter in Zimbabwe supports its controversial involvement. And a worldwide consultative process calls for a stronger, not weaker Programme to Combat Racism (PCR). Some Orthodox talk once again of withdrawing from the Council but they in fact become more involved than ever, and in new areas. Critics accuse the WCC of being taken over by Marxist ideology. Yet a new theological vitality emerges as action/reflection of people from all over the world meet at the WCC to challenge each other's "partial gospel". The human needs of the world overwhelm. And the New International Economic Order (NIEO) slides out of the realm of serious political possibility, at least in simple talk. But the churches dramatically increase their interchurch aid through the WCC, service and aid projects are more often directed at root causes, institutions of the church — schools, hospitals, homes — re-evaluate whom they are serving, and less paternalistic ways of sharing resources are seriously proposed. The gap between the poor and the rich grows. Yet the WCC receives from several directions a new affirmation that the bias of the gospel is indeed for the poor which requires the churches to understand what that solidarity requires. Moral "minorities" and evangelistic crusades and television salesmen divide the gospel and confuse the observers. But the WCC and evangelicals in general move closer to understanding that what we do is as important as what we say, that justice and witness go together. Science and technology seem out of control. Even so serious conversations begin that herald a new science and faith debate replacing the old science against faith problem. The local churches too often remain God's "frozen assets". Yet renewal breaks out in the most unexpected ways, and the Council learns something of that from charismatics, among others.

It is the best and worst of times.

The book

After the work of the Nairobi Assembly, the Central Committee determined four "programme thrusts" for the work of the Council from the welter of recommendations and suggestions that had emerged. They were:
1) the expression and communication of our faith in the triune God;
2) the search for a just, participatory and sustainable society;
3) the unity of the church and its relation to the unity of humankind;
4) education and renewal in search of true community.

I shall make use of these four "thrusts" in describing the journey from Nairobi to Vancouver. It is done partly to organize the mass of material that needs to be presented. But it is also important because the staff and committees take seriously the mandate to address their work in relation to the four "thrusts".

The "thrusts" represent the concerns on which the Council focuses its total work. They include and integrate the special areas on which the programmes of units and sub-units concentrate. The first one, for example, on the expression and communication of the faith, embraces the CWME concern for a credible witness and mission and the Faith and Order concern for a common confession of the faith. In an even broader sense it is the concern of all sub-units. So is unity, and so is renewal. But in the kind of overall survey that is attempted in this book, it is not always possible to do justice to the contribution

14

of all the sub-units to all the four "thrusts". Nor, in a few cases, to the present structure of the Council.

The increasing participation of the Orthodox churches in the work of the Council and the cooperation with Roman Catholics at different levels should perhaps be dealt with in a variety of contexts. I have referred to them in the first chapter, and I hope it is not entirely out of place in the discussion of mission. But it is a much richer story than my brief references indicate. Perhaps it is a story by itself and needs to be fold in full.

* * *

In any case what is written here is the work of a journalist, not a theologian, church official, or veteran of WCC assemblies and committees. It has been my good fortune to have been touched by the ecumenical adventure in my own church experience, in international travel, and in some meetings. The interpretations, the emphases, the mistakes, the omissions are my own and not those of the WCC. I was provided with access and given the freedom to record as I wished. This is written for those who are not insiders by one who is definitely not an insider. What we have in common is the journey of faith.

CHAPTER 1

THE EXPRESSION AND COMMUNICATION OF OUR FAITH IN THE TRIUNE GOD

Towards a missionary movement among the poor

Speaking from 11 years' work among factory workers in Hong Kong, Raymond Fung was reporting "that a case can be made for a missionary movement among the world's poor, particularly the poor in the third world". "I would like to urge the churches", he said, "to help each other so that slum dwellers, factory workers, street labourers and farm hands and their families could be confronted with the claims of Jesus Christ."

Fung, a first-generation Christian and Baptist lay person then employed by the Hong Kong Christian Industrial Committee, was addressing the 1980 Melbourne conference on world mission and evangelism. He said:

> I would like to make a case for a focusing of missionary attention on building evangelizing and witnessing communities of the poor which will discover and live their expressions of faith among the masses of the poor and the oppressed.... There can be no serious understanding of Jesus' mission without reference to his commitment to the poor and the rejected of society. The bias of the ecumenical fellowship towards the poor is no less a strategic step towards the realization of the great commission of Jesus Christ. The reason is a simple matter of numbers.
>
> We cannot be serious, and do not deserve to be taken seriously, if we claim to be interested in global evangelization — of Asia, of Africa, of Latin America — and yet refuse to take as central to our evangelistic commitment the masses of the poor in the cities and villages all over the world. A middle-class church in a sea of peasants and industrial workers makes no sense, theologically and statistically.

Fung reported that out of the Hong Kong Council's sharing of the gospel with the poor, in helping them to understand their rights as workers, in the law courts or protest rallies, or while discussing strategy, reading the Bible and praying together, certain discoveries were made, about themselves, the Christian faith, and the poor. "Men and women are not only wilful violators of God's laws, they are also violated." A person not only sins, but is sinned against.

> There has been too much shallowness in our understanding of sin in the churches' evangelistic enterprises. Could it be that many evangelists of our churches today have no notion of human sinned-againstness?... If that is the case, then no wonder the poor who experience indignity and injustice every day don't give a hoot about evangelism.... The gospel should not only call on people to repent of their sins; it must call on them to resist the forces which sin against them....
> A community of the sinned-against struggling against the forces of sin is an evangelizing context. It is in a community in struggle that evangelism takes place.

The churches are sent into the world "to proclaim by word and deed the gospel of Jesus Christ to the whole world to the end that all may believe" says the constitution of the Commission on World Mission and Evangelism. From the first accounts of the early church in the Book of Acts, the missionary mandate is clear from the expansion of the community of believers. "And day by day the Lord added to their number those whom he was saving" (Acts 2:46-47).

If the "great commission" to "go therefore and make disciples of all nations" (Matt. 28:16) is specific, churches have for some time differed on how to be faithful to that calling.

The road to Melbourne

For two centuries the primary expression of the missionary calling from the churches in the West was evangelism through the foreign missionary boards. To all parts of the world went a remarkable company of men and women as servants of the message of love and reconciliation. The obvious fruits of that historic endeavour are reflected in the churches that share the faith around the world.

But that also presented problems. It tended to identify witness to the gospel with one activity. Missionaries were those who were sent out. Those at home contributed only money to that. The Orthodox were identified as non-missionary and only today — as will be seen later — has communication been restored on mission as practised by the Orthodox. Missionary agencies were set up by a faithful minority independent of the central church structures and often found it difficult to work together and in true partnership with the churches that grew up from their work.

This last concern brought the mission agencies together in the watershed ecumenical event of the century, the 1910 Edinburgh conference. Although at Edinburgh more than 80 per cent of the participants came from the UK and the US (and greetings were sent from King George V and US ex-President Theodore Roosevelt), some third world participants made an impact.

Cheng Ching-Yi of China told the delegates: "Speaking plainly, we hope to see in the near future a united Christian church without any denominational distinctions.... The church of Christ is universal, not only irrespective of denominations, but also irrespective of nationalities."

Edinburgh had surveyed the world in its concern for carrying the gospel but had not, in Potter's words at Melbourne — seventy years later — applied "their prophetic assessment and judgment to the situation of their own countries and churches, except to lament the lukewarmness of Christians as regards the world mission. And yet, the situation in Europe was at that time perilously moving into a cataclysmic conflict."

"The abounding optimism" of Edinburgh was destroyed by the slaughter of World War I. A more sober International Missionary Council emerged in 1921. Mission history can also be read by the conferences held by the IMC and CWME in, yes, such cities as Jerusalem, Tambaram (Madras), Mexico City and Bangkok. The IMC was "in association with the WCC from 1948", which had even then as a function "to support the churches in their task of evangelism".

By 1961 when it was a growing consensus that the task of mission and evangelism should be based in local churches everywhere, the IMC "integrated" with the WCC as the Commission on World Mission and Evangelism. Within the Council, it carries the primary, *but by no means sole,* responsibility for two of the constitutional functions of the WCC: "to facilitate the common witness of the churches in every place and each place" and "to support the churches in their worldwide missionary task".

Indeed within Unit I, these functions are shared with the other subunits. The "visible unity" worked on most specifically by the Subunit on Faith and Order is "in order that the world may believe"; Church and Society's contacts with scientists and technologists can, among other things, be regarded as the church reaching out to talented people sometimes described as "ex-Christians".

Melbourne 1980

The ninth world mission conference in the Edinburgh line met in Melbourne in 1980 under the theme "Your Kingdom Come". The

CWME constitution calls for such a conference between assemblies "to provide opportunities for churches, mission agencies, groups, and national and regional councils concerned with Christian mission, to meet together for reflection and consultation leading to common witness."

Such meetings are useful, says Dr Emilio Castro (Uruguay), CWME Director, not because it is possible to set a global master plan for world evangelization. But world gatherings like Melbourne, Lausanne (the evangelical equivalent), synods of Roman Catholic bishops, and WCC assemblies "are useful and necessary for reciprocal correction and inspiration; sharing experiences; personal encounter; intercessory prayer."

The Melbourne meeting reflected some of the changes in the seventy years since Edinburgh. The 600 participants (250 official delegates) were a diverse, rich mix from more than a hundred countries. The most representative meeting to consider mission in church history, it included a number of evangelicals, 36 Roman Catholics (many integrally involved; at the 1963 Mexico City conference the two Catholics were observers), over 50 Orthodox, and about 60 participants from urban and rural mission projects around the world.

One change was quite obvious. These words from one of the reports: "The concept of mission being from 'sending' to 'receiving' countries has long been replaced by a mutuality in shared mission involving a two-way flow between the churches in the industrialized countries and the so-called third world."

Melbourne seems likely to be remembered as the mission conference where the gospel's bias for the poor, as demonstrated repeatedly in the ministry of Jesus who preached "the good news to the poor", was most clearly affirmed.

It is important to emphasize that those who planned the agenda and those who attended began with the question of what it means for the church to be faithful in the stewardship of the gospel in the current historical period. They did not begin — as the WCC is often accused of doing — with questions of poverty, war, inequality, ecology and the like. They did not ask first how the church can help the poor but rather, what are the implications of world poverty for the mission of the Church?

The WCC is often criticized for its failure to be concerned about the "unreached", the vast numbers of people said to be outside the reach of the churches on the six continents. The Rev. Harvey Hoekstra, who has served as a missionary with the US Church of the Brethren (a WCC member), wrote a book in 1978 (before

Melbourne, which he attended) called *The World Council of Churches and the Demise of Evangelism.* Hoekstra's thoughtful critique — a welcome contrast to some of the vitriol unleashed in recent years — suggests that the IMC was swallowed up by the WCC and that the churches no longer receive the support they need to "reach the unreached". Hoekstra believes that the WCC has developed a new definition of mission primarily concerned to work for a better society with emphasis on human dignity and human rights.

> Such participation in the social struggle is a worthy objective as long as it does not lead to the eclipse or neglect of the churches' responsibility to win others to faith in Christ. But this has often been the result. Rather than giving member churches "support... in their worldwide missionary and evangelistic task," WCC programmes have too often tended to divert those churches from that task.

The Melbourne meeting entered this debate. It seemed to be saying that the poor are the vast majority of the "unreached" (a term CWME does not use since God may reach where the visible instruments of the church do not, or because some are reached and reject the message because of the way it is presented).

In what ways does "the expression and communication of the faith in the Triune God" come to the poor with integrity? "Evangelism is true and credible only when it is both word and deed: proclamation and witness. To say this is not to suggest that evangelism derives its power from the good deeds of Christians; our failures in obedience, however, can act as stumbling blocks."

And from one of the four section reports, *Good News to the Poor:*

> The churches will need to surrender their attitudes of benevolence and charity by which they have condescended to the poor; in many cases this will mean a radical change in the institutional life of the missionary movement. The churches will also need to be ready to listen to the poor, so that they can hear the gospel from the poor, as well as learn about the ways in which they have helped to make them poor.

But the credibility of that proclamation depends upon the "authenticity of the total witness of the church".

Melbourne perceived a "change in the direction of mission" with the "poor" churches of the world as the bearers of mission: world mission and evangelism may now be primarily in their hands.

CWME's and CICARWS's joint desk carrying responsibilities for the Ecumenical Sharing of Personnel (ESP) have together organized small regional consultations in Latin America, Asia and the Caribbean to explore this perception and see what this might mean for the world church in its sharing of personnel in mission.

A recent document from Lima, Peru, discusses the increased sense of mission within the Catholic church which has helped in "the re-evangelization of great sectors of the continent". But the church must also have a mission outside, it says.

In a short time, half of the Catholics in the world will be in Latin America in a world composed of 20 per cent Catholics. For Asia and Africa, the Latin American churches in the third millenium will be the most valid intermediaries and evangelizers. This is not simply because of the number of Christians, but "also because of their being in a 'brother' continent: poor, and without the old colonialization pretensions.... there is no incompatibility between being in need and receiving missionaries".

What Melbourne did, says Emilio Castro, is to help solidify an understanding that cuts across the usual differences in the church. In their deliberations, evangelicals are more certain about the call to social justice. WCC members are not reluctant to talk of evangelism, a willingness to testify in the world to their faith. "It is not possible to have an evangelistic attitude without a concern for social justice. And it is not possible for Christians to engage in liberation struggles or development efforts without the obligation to say why they are involved. It is acting in the name and the naming of the action."

Other tasks

CWME has many other responsibilities. If mission and evangelism are in fact no longer to be seen as something delegated to specialists for which the average church member pays, how do the churches respond? In the 1960s CWME initiated a study on the missionary structures of the congregation, focusing on challenging those structures which are too rigid for the new mission understanding. Now, through workshops and sharing of experiences (the *International Review of Mission (IRM),* a serious quarterly on mission which has been published for seventy years, carries some of those items; a more popular version, a monthly called *The Evangelism Newsletter,* has a growing list of subscribers), it is helping churches to work on how motivation and awareness of the local church as the advance guard of mission can be enhanced. One interesting method has been to invite international teams to visit a national church for an in-depth review of mission procedures and attitudes.

Another issue of interest is how mission and evangelism are to be reported in church publications. Traditionally, mission reporting was a form of public relations with fund-raising as the first goal. But if the purpose now is to animate the whole church for mission, how is that communicated? CWME has held sessions with religious journalists to work on this problem.

CWME has invited mission agencies to discuss their vocation jointly. Because they are no longer the centre of the mission enterprise but in partnership with very active churches, they are seeking together to find a new role in the total missionary response of the church. One way is by engagement with the newly emerging mission reality of their own situation. More than one million Turks now live and work in the Federal Republic of Germany. How does an agency that used to have foreign missions in Muslim areas address that? What of the new multi-racial societies of England, France? How is the mission vocation developed in socialist countries where employment and housing may be more adequate but spiritual malaise self-evident?

Common Witness, a study document of the Joint Working Group of the Roman Catholic Church and the World Council of Churches, was published in 1981 "as the result of several years' labour and the collection and analysis of reports of actual experience in common witness". CWME and the Secretariat for Promoting Christian Unity (RC) published the booklet jointly.

The document contains numerous examples of common witness. In the words of the introduction, the theses elaborated in it "are born of the unity found in engagement in mission to the world, that cradle of the ecumenical movement".

Mission amidst struggles

CWME, and all of WCC, continues to be energized by the involvement with urban and rural mission. The URM office has enabled small groups of people struggling in their local situations and testifying to their faith to find each other, to be in communication with each other, across national and regional lines.

Their stories are an important form of theological reflection and are often shared. According to the Rev. George Todd (USA) — he is secretary for URM, with Samuel Kobia (Kenya) — the stories do not idealize the work of these groups. "On the contrary, they reflect the anxieties and frustrations of what is being attempted. Some work may appear quite ordinary, but takes on special significance when viewed in a context of severe political repression. Some stories tell of humble church initiatives to make contact with people in their societies who are the victims of injustice. At some point there is authentic participation in the suffering of the people and their struggle to become subjects of their own history. It is in that struggle that the meaning of the cross and the resurrection becomes very real."

The story from South Korea is one of the most exciting and terrible and long-running. Urban Industrial Mission (UIM) emerged in the Korean churches more than twenty years ago at a time when more than 80 per cent of Korea's people lived in rural areas. Pastoral care for the early waves of those working in factories was much needed. As Korean economic policy concentrated on manufacturing for export, waves of workers were pushed towards the factories in the cities. Today its urban labour pool is about 25 per cent of the total population.

A UIM report says it was during this period in the late 1960s that the Korean church "really assumed full responsibility for industrial mission and tried to solve problems together with the workers, putting a stress on the educational role of the church in reaffirming the dignity and humanity of the workers".

UIM offices near the factories served as meeting places, offered pastoral care for workers in a harsh environment and helped them organize their working conditions. One girl — 750,000 are estimated to work in textile plants alone, most under the age of 22 — reported: "At the beginning when I entered the factory, work was so hard that I often wept. However, the other workers only cared about whether they fulfilled their own quota and the atmosphere was very cold. But my friends at the factory who were UIM members were very understanding. So I came to know that the atmosphere in UIM is really warm compared to the cold factory surroundings."

The government and the factory owners were extremely unhappy to have interference in their operations. One UIM document says that informing people, "especially those who are poor and have little education, of their real circumstances" apparently is threatening to those in power "all over the world, Korea being no exception".

Pressures escalated. Countless UIM-related persons were arrested and often tortured. Heavy special taxes were levied, offices raided and records seized. Foreign missionaries related to UIM work were harassed and sometimes deported.

The story and its drama could be told at great length. Let it suffice to end with a few quotes from an article which appeared in the *Christian Conference of Asia News* a few years ago:

The church is growing in Korea. The gospel is being preached and people are turning to Jesus Christ.... The church is also suffering in Korea. Several ministers of the gospel are in prison, together with a great many others, including students, professors, journalists and others.

... These are not criminals in the usual understanding of the term. They are people who have dared to ask, or even simply pray to God, for the restoration of the ordinary freedoms of a civilized democratic country: the right to speak freely, to vote in free elections, to strike for better working conditions, to enjoy a press that can speak the truth. These are people for whom the mission of the church includes the struggle to create a society where everyone can live, serve, love and worship freely and without fear before God.

Orthodox involvement

It is said that in no ecumenical meeting have the Orthodox been present in larger numbers and participated more fully than at Melbourne. That surprised some people because so much of the Orthodox contribution has been within the theological and doctrinal discussions of Faith and Order in previous years.

In the years since Nairobi an interesting process has been set in motion by CWME to help overcome some of the misunderstandings about the meaning of mission both by the Orthodox and other churches who have referred to the Orthodox as non-missionary churches. In a major contribution to ecumenical thought, *Martyria/Mission: the Witness of the Orthodox Churches Today,* Prof. Ion Bria (Romania) of the CWME Orthodox desk explains why mission has presented a problem:

> Too often the word "mission" has meant penetration by the non-Orthodox missionary agencies into the traditional Orthodox territory in order to convert Orthodox believers.... This is a permanent source of tension among Christians.... "Foreign missions" simply denotes non-Orthodox faith, and a Catholic or Protestant mission working in an Orthodox area is considered by the Orthodox as an ecclesiological contradiction.

Since Nairobi, Bria has worked with the Orthodox to begin to express mission in their own terms. Much of this work has taken place in a series of consultations on mission held — in 1974 in Bucharest, Etchmiadzin (Armenia) in 1975, Prague in 1976, Paris in 1978, Cairo in 1979, and Zica (Yugoslavia) in 1980.

The first step in this process was the recognition of the early missionary outreach of the apostolic eastern centres which spread the gospel across Asia Minor, to the Arabs in the south, to North Africa

25

and Asia and the conversion of much of Russia in 981. It was without question the repression under centuries of Ottoman Turk domination which brought an end to this form of missionary outreach and a concentration on preserving and defending the faith in their own countries. Even today Orthodox churches are often minorities in Islamic or socialist societies.

The consultations were able for the first time to involve parish priests and people beyond the religious hierarchy and theological faculties usually involved in the WCC. For example, in Yugoslavia in 1980 a consultation called "Preaching and Teaching Christian Faith Today" considered the "priest's ministry of teaching and preaching", "the proclamation of the gospel", "liturgical language and culture", and the "liturgical community as basis for evangelization and education for mission".

The 1979 consultation was on the "Missionary Vocation of the Monastic Orders", and was an effort to understand the mission implications of the monastic life, especially in a world increasingly attracted to the idea of pilgrimage to places of reflection and meditation.

In the process the Orthodox have begun to make more clear the mission implications of the liturgy to those from other confessions. The liturgy with its participation in the saving act of God through Jesus Christ is itself a proclamation. The worshipping community itself is an act of witness.

Increasingly in the Orthodox discussion of witness and mission the phrase "liturgy after the liturgy" has come into play. As Ion Bria writes in the introduction to *Martyria/Mission:* "Eucharist is the source of church life and mission, the inner stimulus which motivated the community for mission. Thus the Liturgy must not be a closed event limited to the celebration in the church and to the nominal members of the church; it has to be continued in the lives of the faithful in all dimensions of life. One cannot separate Liturgy and life; therefore there is a liturgy after Liturgy."

CHAPTER 2

THE SEARCH FOR A JUST, PARTICIPATORY AND SUSTAINABLE SOCIETY

A concern that cuts across the Council

This emphasis, fortunately, can be shortened to JPSS, as it is known by those who work with it. But unlike the other three emphases, JPSS will require some explanation.

JPSS was, and remains, more of a vision than a programme reality. And even that vision is not easy to capture on paper. The advisory committee appointed to help articulate the search for the JPSS discovered this when its 20-page presentation to the 1979 Central Committee was "received without approval". Something about the theological expression of people's participation in the messianic kingdom sounded strange to traditionalists, said one person who was there, although others thought it was one of the most important contributions yet from third world contextual theology at this level of the WCC. It is still available and worth reading. The introduction provides the context for the JPSS:

> Throughout its history, the ecumenical movement has sought to reflect not only on the unity and mission of the church, but also on the basic Christian convictions which could guide the people of God in the struggle for a better society. It was not an arbitrary decision when, in 1976, the Central Committee adopted the search for a "Just, Participatory and Sustainable Society" as one of four major programme emphases for the work of the Council.

The purpose is not to "present a blueprint or a Christian programme of an ideal society". Rather the search begins from present history which differs from region to region, with an increasing number of societies "characterized by structures of injustice, lack of participation, and the threat of unsustainability".

Participation locally is essential but it must be made global to deal with root causes. One encouragement comes from movements of people challenging structures of alienating power.

The Central Committee in 1979 called for further reflection on

JPSS in upcoming world conferences, which occurred in at least four. And it called for a study of political ethics.

The 1979 advisory committee report noted the "sometimes conflicting claims of sustainability and social justice" in the regions. The central concern of people in Africa, Asia and Latin America is "justice in terms of the realization of primary economic and social needs.... The internal problems and conflicts in many countries are exacerbated by foreign political, economic and military intervention."

In much of the northern hemisphere sustainability appears central "in terms of the needs for industrial redeployment, self-reliance in the use of raw materials, alternatives to the present options for energy and military technology, and solutions to structural unemployment".

In regions of the southern hemisphere urgency is placed on the "sustenance or sustainability of life", while in socialist nations the priority is maintenance of peace without which sustainability is inconceivable.

Since 1980, Dr Koson Srisang (Thailand), who has other duties within CCPD (Commission on the Churches' Participation in Development), has been involved in the study of political ethics called for by the Central Committee. The late 1981 Cyprus meeting marked the conclusion of one phase of this study.

The JPSS study has had difficulty focusing, all admit. *One World* asked Philip Potter why it had seemed to overwhelm so many separate parts of the ecumenical movement.

(That) is itself a justification for the search. It's so difficult to cope with because we have kept so many things in compartments.

Take the two important words, "participation" and "sustainability". They do go together, despite all the efforts to prove they don't. For example, the world population will be six billion by the end of the century. That means we'll have vast human resources but our natural resources are increasingly limited.

So what do you do? How do you use and share those natural resources? Who decides? Today very few people take part in decision-making, very few enjoy the natural resources. And what's more, these resources are largely used for destructive purposes.

Various sub-units, nevertheless, have been very conscious of the JPSS concern in their work. It has cut across the Council. But those discussed in this chapter have a particular relationship.

Church and Society

Science and the JPSS debate

"The ways of the church are sometimes a little roundabout," Prof. Enilo Ajakaiye told the WCC Central Committee in 1980. The Nigerian scientist had attended the 1979 (MIT) conference on the contribution of faith, science and technology in the struggle for a just, participatory and sustainable society, but wasn't quite sure how she got an invitation. Still, she went. And testified that it added a new dimension to her "responsibilities as a Christian and a scientist".

Through her, the conference also made some impact on Nigerian colleagues. One, a Muslim scientist, took a copy of the MIT report home for the night and the next day asked how he could get a copy. "I didn't know you Christians were concerned about questions such as science and technology."

It worried Dr Ajakaiye that her church has not yet dealt with such questions although "Nigerian communities are being overwhelmed by modern technology, whether in petroleum or mining or rapid industrial developments."

Nigerians, she believes, are very much aware of the "good" aspects of science and technology: new drugs curing tropical diseases, fertilizers increasing food production, jet planes reducing the distances, better building materials for houses.

> But there is another side to the coin. Rapid technological development also means waste and abuse of the environment. Some of our Nigerian rivers and lakes are polluted with oil spillages. Forests are fast disappearing. At least 30,000 tons of gas are flared (burned at the wells) daily due to technological and economic considerations. These all mean that local people are not only being deprived of an adequate supply of protein, good drinking water and food, healthy and scenic environments, but they also have to change their life-styles. Fishermen can no longer go fishing, and arable farmlands are so scorched that farmers cannot till the land. In Nigeria, for example, environmental problems associated with oil exploration have led to a phenomenal increase in various diseases.

Dr Ajakaiye was concerned that a large proportion of the people of the world still live in terrible poverty and malnutrition despite advances in science and technology. Moreover, "a vast part of modern scientific and technological research is spent preparing new military weapons".

30

Ninety per cent of all the scientists who have ever lived are alive today, go the oft-quoted statistics, 94 per cent of them work in the developed countries, and half of that 94 per cent work on military-related research. "There can obviously be no justice (or) peace as long as such an unjust division of the world's technological power and capacities exists."

The churches, Ajakaiye urges, "can and should make a substantial contribution to the thinking of our communities" regarding a just and participatory use of science and technology. To do this, they will need the "help of the scientists within their midst who can give them a larger understanding of the requirements of a humanly-based technology policy.... There is no more urgent task for the WCC..."

What Prof. Ajakaiye did so well in her speech was to illustrate from her own perspective precisely what the WCC had been charged to do by the Nairobi Assembly and the 1976 Central Committee: work through the Sub-unit on Church and Society (C&S) on the theological, social and ethical dimensions of modern science and technology as they relate to the JPSS debate. A major conference was to be the focal event for the work.

The faith and science debate

Church and Society is an inheritor of the Life and Work tradition which recognized in Stockholm in 1925 the hope for "a just and fraternal order, through which the opportunity shall be assured for the development, according to God's design, of the full manhood of all".

The 1966 Geneva conference, organized by C&S, on "Christians in the Social and Technical Revolutions of our Time", was a major event in WCC history. But, as has often been pointed out, the church was better able there to discuss social than technical revolutions. Out of 450 participants, only a handful were bona fide scientists or technologists.

Ecumenical social thought to that time had been largely undertaken by some dedicated theologians, ethicists, economists, sociologists, politicians, political scientists, businessmen and trade unionists. Over the past decade, C&S has attempted to engage in conversation those actively involved in science and technology.

Which is not as simple as it sounds. Science has long threatened the church, as Galileo, Copernicus and Darwin, among others, discovered. Scientists are often, in the words of long-time C&S Director Dr Paul Abrecht (USA), "ex-Christians, people motivated by their faith to go into scientific fields in order to serve but who had found the church uninterested in, if not hostile to, what they were doing. Consequently they often have drifted to the margin of the churches. They have to be convinced that the church is seeking understanding of such issues as gene splicing, amniocentesis and selective abortion, and that it does not enter the discussion with its mind already made up.''

No sooner had C&S started its work in 1970 on the theme of "The Future of Man and Society in a World of Science-Based Technology", than the optimism about science and technology was called into sharp question. This began with questions about sustainability. Abrecht recalls particularly the 1971 and 1972 working group meetings which included contributions from Jørgen Randers of Norway, a co-author of *Limits to Growth,* and E.F. Schumacher, author of *Small is Beautiful,* neither of which had been published at that time. While they had sharp disagreements with each other, they both argued the then new thesis that the world could not maintain its present growth in production and consumption.

The thesis was and continues to be sharply debated, as do the political implications. The working committee, in the words of Prof. Roger Shinn of New York's Union Theological Seminary, "has insisted that ecology must not become the new fad of people bored with social justice and seeking an escape from its demands. It has argued that any notion of limits on production makes more urgent the requirements of just distribution, not only of consumer goods but also of the economic power of production." After Nairobi C&S began to move towards a world conference on "Faith, Science and the Future", to take place in July 1979 at the Massachusetts Institute of Technology (MIT) near Boston. In preparation for this and to further the dialogue between scientists and theologians it organized a series of specialized meetings. Among them: genetics and the quality of life; science and theology; nuclear energy; political economy, ethics and theology. Several publications came from this process, including *The Human Presence: an Orthodox View of Nature* (Paulos Gregorios), *Facing up to Nuclear Power* (John Francis and Paul Abrecht), a conference preparatory study volume, *Faith, Science and the Future: the Liberation of Life* (Charles Birch and John Cobb), and a number of issues of *Anticipation,* the sub-unit's bulletin. Shinn wrote that the 1979 conference was a culmination of one set of activities and "a germinal occasion for new programmes still to be defined".

The 13-day study conference created new interest in university and church circles. The original plan was for a conference of about

350 people; almost 900 came to the event, with 405 official participants from 56 countries (of whom 91 were students). This time the scientists and technologists were out in full force. The climate had changed. No one can recall as diverse an ecumenical event in the church's history.

As Philip Potter said in the opening address, the churches are now more open to these discussions and the scientists are more modest about their claims. "Scientists are much more conscious of their social responsibility than in the past. Indeed, it is they who are posing acute ethical questions for the churches and theologians."

In his introduction to the first volume of the MIT report, *Faith and Science in an Unjust World,* Roger Shinn noted that, along with sharp disagreements, he found three points of consensus.

He found no scientific utopians. Different degrees of help were expected from various research and development programmes. "But there appeared to be universal recognition that the world's major problems require changes in social structures and in the values and commitments embodied in those problems."

Nor was anyone "confident of a 'religious fix' for the basic social problems of this century.... There was no claim that the churches were able to tell the scientists the ethical formulas that would make their work benign."

Finally, scientists did not confront theologians as groups. "In the big debates — and there were some — scientists and theologians stood together on *both* sides of the issue."

Shinn also described, in what he called over-simplified terms, the emergence of two pictures of science at the conference. In one, science is a way of seeking knowledge and a method to solve problems. It can be misused. "But the glory of true science is to keep alive the quest for understanding."

In the other, science is seen as power in the hands of the already powerful at the expense of the weak. "Science and scientific technologies are forces that protect privilege, impose oppression, and in our experience have inflicted pain and death."

MIT's Prof. Jonathan King told the 1980 Central Committee that the conference was important in "bridging the gaps between those in the church concerned about the impact of science and technology on human society, and those of us in the scientific and technical sphere who are worried about the uses and misuses of our labours".

He also gave testimony to a new element in this work. The conference was his "first experience in working with people who were actually concerned over the plight of the world's people, and it was an invaluable experience''.

But he also warned of the task ahead, saying the conference had made only the slightest impression on the thousands who work at MIT, "scientists and engineers who supervise the expenditures of tens of millions of dollars on research, all under the eyes of the world's largest and most powerful corporations, and tied to the world's largest and most powerful military machine''.

Someone wrote on a graffiti board at MIT that "to have a conference on technology and a just society at MIT is like having a conference on disarmament at the Pentagon''. To which someone else added: "Or God becoming human.''

What the MIT meeting symbolizes is a new faith and science debate. Scientists and theologians are together questioning the worldview of rational scientific assurance rather than wasting time on the old questions like evolution (although recent right-wing attempts in the US to push "creationism'' into the biology curriculum in schools does raise echoes of the old "faith versus science'' era).

After MIT

The questions now are, where are we going? What is the end use of this knowledge? Can we cope with this power? How is it to be made universal rather than the property of the industrial nations? Why have capitalism and socialism put so much faith in science and technology? What kind of society do we want?

Some groups formed after MIT have continued to address these and many other questions. A few churches have begun to take advantage of the scientific resources within their own congregations. But how churches move to engage these issues — issues of a just, sustainable and participatory society — is still being worked out and will perhaps receive serious attention at Vancouver. The challenge is there. One section at MIT dealt with the economics of JPSS. It concluded that the concept cannot be dismembered into "justice for the third world, participation for the second world and sustainability for the first world. We of the human race are all members of one another. We must together struggle to extend participation, develop sustainability, and to let justice roll down like waters and righteousness like an ever-flowing stream'' (Amos 5:24).

C&S itself has continued to devote its attention to these issues. In fact in 1980 its working group suggested to the Central Committee that its name should be changed to "Faith, Science and Society'', or "Church, Science and Society'' to make clear its function and express "a continuing concern of the WCC in the coming years beyond the next assembly" in science and technology which play a crucial role in shaping society and human thought. It would also clear up confusions about what it can undertake as a sub-unit. The Central Committee, noting the long ecumenical history associated with the current name, delayed a decision until further discussion.

Nuclear hearing — and "Energy for my Neighbour"

One example of direct follow-up was the International Public Hearing on Nuclear Weapons and Disarmament held in late 1981 in Amsterdam. (History often sets an unexpected stage for WCC meetings. The nuclear hearing began the day after an estimated 400,000 anti-nuclear protesters gathered in Amsterdam. The erratic US Sky-lab deposited its litter over Australia as MIT got underway. The CWME Melbourne meeting was in session when the Chinese fired a test ICBM into Pacific waters, further angering Pacific Islanders who protest French nuclear testing in the area.)

The issue of nuclear disarmament and the conversion from military technology to socially useful purposes arose from the floor at MIT under the leadership of scientists. It became an unscheduled plenary where the combined groups acknowledged "with penitence the part played by science in the development of weapons of mass destruction and the failure of the churches to oppose it", and now pleaded "with the nations of the world for the reduction and eventual abolition of such weapons".

C&S jointly organized the nuclear hearing with the Commission of the Churches on International Affairs (CCIA) which has long had this issue on its agenda. A distinguished panel of 17 Christians condemned the limited nuclear war concept "unreservedly" and called nuclear deterrence an "unacceptable" basis for peace. The purpose of the hearing — which heard testimony from 37 expert witnesses from various fields, different political perspectives, and all parts of the world — was to consider the problems posed by escalation of the nuclear arms race and changing concepts of nuclear war.

C&S has had a longer involvement in the rapidly changing world of biology, producing as early as 1973 (from a consultation) a book on *Genetics and the Quality of Life*. A section at MIT, "Ethical Issues in the Biological Manipulation of Life", called for a working group on the benefits, threats and hazards of human genetic engineering.

Such a group met in 1981 and reported that for some people such new technologies as amniocentesis, genetic screening, selective abortion, *in vitro* fertilization (test-tube babies), artificial insemination, surrogate motherhood and gene transplantation challenge "historic Christian teaching about the dignity of human life and the way this is to be expressed. Fear and distrust have greeted the call for a new understanding of life."

The working group stated that the church is "challenged to ensure that human life is enriched and human society made more whole.... (This) requires study and reflection on the new knowledge that biology brings, and the working out of the relation between faith and this knowledge to an extent we have as yet hardly begun."

The energy crisis is another complex problem of social justice and sustainability about which C&S has been concerned. Initially special attention was focused on nuclear energy, with people of widely diverging positions debating the issue. A 1978 report stated that nuclear energy is "a conditional good, subject to reasoned acceptance under some circumstances and to reasoned rejection in others". The issue was hotly debated at the MIT conference as well, which was undoubtedly influenced by the accident at the Three Mile Island nuclear reactor in Pennsylvania, USA, three months prior to the conference. The majority of the participants voted for a limited, five-year moratorium on the construction of new nuclear power plants, in order to gain time to discuss the overall costs, risks and benefits of nuclear energy.

In the meantime a special programme of C&S on "Energy for my Neighbour" began a major enquiry into the ethical, social and political aspects of the energy crisis from the point of view of the 2,000 million people of the developing countries, for whom the dwindling supplies of firewood and agricultural residues, their principal fuel, are much more pressing than the concern of the industrialized world over the depletion of petroleum reserves. A number of regional consultations in Asia, Latin America and Africa on the theme "Towards More Just and Sustainable Energy Development" have led to a better understanding of these issues as well as of the responsibility of the churches in this area. The results of this enquiry will be presented to the Vancouver Assembly.

Commission of the Churches on International Affairs
The seminar, held at the UN Headquarters in New York, addressed the relations that exist between human rights, peace and development. Reading from hasty notes rather than a formal document, Dwain Epps (USA), Director of the UN HQ Liaison Office for the CCIA, responded at one point during the discussions.

Previous speakers had cited the notorious imbalance between military spending and official development assistance in the industrialized world, as well as the growing expenditure in many developing countries on military matters. Member states of the UN have repeatedly been urged to reduce military budgets and transfer these savings to development assistance. (If this has ever happened, it has escaped public attention.)

Epps pointed to the increasing documentation demonstrating that investments in arms production are inflationary, intensify unemployment, and the technology created — contrary to myth — is difficult to convert to civilian production. "Arms production and transfers are, therefore, disastrous for all nations, rich and poor, heightening the economic threats to peace and survival of all peoples, and threatening the implementation of fundamental human rights." He went on to speak of the link between militarization and human rights, and of the worship by military regimes of the idol of national security. His remarks reflected some of the emphases developed in the work of the CCIA in the past decade. CCIA's mandate includes the "analysis and interpretation of political events and developments" and advice to the Council on "the formulation of policies regarding political issues".

CCIA's concerns flow, at least indirectly, from a long history traced to the participation of an ecumenical group of church people at the Second Hague Peace Conference in 1907. Among other things, this group called for an end to the arms race and for arbitration in international disputes. An ensuing organization, the World Alliance for Promoting International Friendship through the Churches, was a primary instrument used in preparing for the Stockholm Life and Work Conference in 1925.

The issue of war and peace remained a dominant theme as the WCC (in the process of formation) lived through the trauma of World War II. The CCIA's direct history comes from the 1948 founding of the WCC, jointly existing between the WCC and the IMC (International Missionary Council) with its key offices related to the UN in New York and in London. The CCIA took an active part in the drafting of major UN documents such as the Universal Declaration of Human Rights and the two international covenants on human rights.

In the 1960s, after the IMC integrated with the WCC, the CCIA gradually shifted its main office to Geneva. The style changed also. Able Westerners who had access to high Western officials and ran a somewhat independent "foreign office" retired, and were succeeded by a broader geographical representation, symbolized by the designation of Leopoldo Niilus (Argentina) as Director in 1969. He was succeeded in 1981 by Ninan Koshy (India), who joined the staff in 1974.

The 1960s, as highlighted in the WCC's life by the Uppsala Assembly, brought to the CCIA, as to other WCC sub-units and ecumenical agencies, a new understanding of its involvements. Disarmament, for example, had been viewed as a specialized undertaking among nations. The WCC through the CCIA tried to influence those negotiations. The message, at least implicitly, to lay people was, these are technical and complicated; leave them to the experts. But as the WCC became more engaged with the life of local churches around the world, new perceptions arose. Statements on disarmament or human rights, however well designed, were important but not the end. Support, challenge, learning from the engagement of the churches where they are, became much more important in the work of the CCIA.

Three emphases of recent years will reflect this approach: human rights, public policy, and the programme for Disarmament and against Militarism and the Arms Race.

This jaw-breaker — second only to Just, Participatory and Sustainable Society in the WCC lexicon — was mandated by the 1979 Central Committee and, when unravelled, identifies a complex of concerns.

Work on militarism

From Nairobi CCIA was directed to work on militarism and it set about defining the term with the crucial help of people living under clear examples of militarism. Classical definitions were inadequate because they usually implied the rise of Bonapartism, German imperial strength, or Japanese military plans for a "co-prosperity sphere". Nor was it to be extended simply to include "banana republics". People began to understand the internal dimensions of militarism (CCIA finds militarization a more descriptive term for today). For example, concern in the USA grew, not just about arming against the Soviet Union, but what the emphasis on arms was doing to the economy and general life.

One illustration of this new understanding comes from *Iron Hand, Velvet Glove: Studies on Militarization in Five Critical Areas of the Philippines,* prepared by the Ecumenical Movement for Justice and Peace in the Philippines and published by the CCIA in 1980 after it was suppressed in the Philippines. "This collection of studies is our first attempt to present a view of how militarization and development are inextricably related in the Filipino situation," the ecumenical group said in its introduction. The Filipino group outlines the deterioration of the economy — to boost it was a primary justification for the imposition of martial law in 1972 — and the growing instability of the Philippines. The study dramatically challenges the claim that militarization has brought national security and development, by concentrating on five areas of the country.

Another significant finding of the CCIA's studies of militarization is the military flourishing that occurs in areas of the third world when transnational corporations arrive to harvest natural resources. The 1977 consultation on militarism also commented on this:

> Often the support of repressive regimes is motivated by economic concerns, particularly the protection and advancement of transnational corporations. For this to happen, efforts are promoted to ensure conditions of "law and order", a task generally entrusted to the military and police of the underdeveloped country most often closely allied with the national elites.

But the stress on the local impact of the arms race does not obscure the mounting alarm about the new situation with nuclear arms. For some years the world had evidenced an uneasy nonchalance about nuclear weapons: they are too destructive to use. But with new doctrines of "limited nuclear warfare" enunciated by those that possess the weapons, the probabilities of nuclear war have increased dramatically. This has produced an electric response in Western Europe, the probable playing field for an initial exchange. It has made statements like that of the 1979 Central Committee which cited "the need for concerted attention to be given to nuclear disarmament especially in nuclear weapon-producing countries" much less isolated than they would have appeared a few years ago.

This mounting concern, which also found strong voice in the C&S MIT meeting, led to the 1981 hearing on nuclear weapons (described earlier) jointly organized by CCIA and C&S.

CCIA is encouraged by various efforts in the churches to "get into" this whole issue. The churches were involved in the European protests of hundreds of thousands of people in late 1981; the biannual meeting of the FRG (Federal Republic of Germany) churches in the Kirchentag (Day of the Churches) in 1981 brought a major statement against current nuclear arms strategy; the Pacific Conference of Churches fights the continued testing of nuclear weapons in the Pacific by the French; the Presbyterian Church in the USA now has a special emphasis on "peace-making".

But it is of concern that new theological perspectives have not yet emerged. The old debate between pacifism and "just war" is no longer an adequate framework. The Archbishop of Canterbury said not long ago that "there is no such thing as just mutual obliteration". Pacifism has new problems with how to engage the role of one's own nation in the more subtle militarization which destroys development possibilities.

A 1978 CCIA conference on disarmament summed it up like this:

> Never before has the human race been as close as it is now to total self-destruction. Today's arms race is an unparalleled waste of human and material resources; it aids repression and violates human rights; it promotes violence and insecurity in place of the security in whose name it is undertaken; it frustrates humanity's aspirations for justice and peace; it has no part in God's designs for his world; it is demonic... To hope in Christ is neither to be complacent about survival nor powerless in the fear of annihilation by the forces of evil but to open our eyes to the transcendent reality of Christ in history.

Human rights

By the beginning of the 1970s the public definitions of human rights were generally in place. Constitutions in most countries enshrined them. The concern now was turning the attention of the churches to the "question how best to implement the standards established".

Careful work in prior consultations, and the moving testimony of individual Christians who had suffered by putting their faith on the line, led Nairobi to confirm the new ecumenical consensus on human rights. Human rights are not to be treated in isolation, they are political in nature, and they are fundamentally a struggle for liberation of an entire community. The earlier WCC emphasis on religious liberty provided a point of departure for a more integral approach to human rights. This was a problem of both participation and justice.

The CCIA is convinced that the main resource available to the WCC, in work with human rights as elsewhere, is the membership. The 1979 Central Committee said:

> ...those who live within any given location are best qualified to interpret and analyze their own experience and best able to prescribe strategies for the realization of human rights within their own situation. It also implies that human rights are nowhere perfectly assured, and that concern abroad must be tempered by a realistic appraisal of responsibility at home.
>
> (But) ecumenical solidarity (calls on the community) to support each other morally, materially and politically.... many churches live in situa-

tions so grave they cannot cope with the problems using their own resources alone... help must be sought by those in need, and must not be imposed, however well meant, from the outside.

An international human rights advisory group — chaired by Indonesian Yap Thiam Hien — met twice during the post-Nairobi period to help solidify the churches' understanding of their responsibilities. The group reaffirmed the understanding of human rights arrived at during the assembly at Nairobi that individual and social rights are interdependent.

While the primary work of the Council on human rights has been through member churches and councils, it has, of course, made direct interventions itself on behalf of groups and individuals. One exception has been the Human Rights Resources Office for Latin America, staffed by the Rev. Charles Harper (USA). Since the Chile crisis of 1974, and in the absence until recently of a regional organization of churches in Latin America, this office has had the role of helping to support those in difficult situations in the volatile political climate in several Latin American countries.

Some delegates to Nairobi had been concerned about restrictions on religious freedom and intellectual dissent in the socialist states of Eastern Europe, especially in the USSR. The Helsinki Declaration, affirming the interdependence of rights — social, economic, cultural, civil and political — contained in the Universal Declaration and the international covenants on human rights, had been signed just before Nairobi. Representatives from member churches in East and West whose governments had signed the Helsinki accords were brought together by the WCC in 1976 to discuss their meaning and observation.

Public policy

The WCC, one friendly observer believes, played a lively and continuing role through its work in public policy at the points of crisis during the period since Nairobi. This is most easily grasped by examining the statements issued by the Central and Executive Committees and by the General Secretary. (Collections exist of the statements, in three volumes, in small books called *The Churches in International Affairs*.)

But the Council reacts in a variety of ways, not simply through public statements and communications to churches and governments. Each year Philip Potter meets with several heads of state. In recent years four ministers for religious affairs from Eastern Europe have visited the WCC. This is an important form of interpretation of the international dimensions of the Christian fellowship. Delegations from member churches are organized to make "pastoral visits" to churches and individuals under stress. Observer teams have also been organized. This is an ongoing and demanding staff function, especially of the CCIA who often do the preparatory work.

Much of the work is never seen by the public. China, for example, is closely monitored. The Chinese church was a founding member of the WCC, and the membership was never formally withdrawn. In 1980 public expression of Christianity was again possible in China and a Chinese Christian Council (CCC) was formed by Protestants. In measured fashion some bilateral relations have been restored, including the visit by six members of the CCC to Hong Kong in 1981 to meet with the Christian Conference of Asia and Hong Kong churches. Will the Chinese church join the Council? The WCC, after all, called early on for the admission of the People's Republic of China to the UN. But the decision is for the Chinese church. In the meantime, the WCC waits, carefully monitoring the political and religious situation in China.

Or another silent act. A friend, who asked not to be identified, told of the time he was under pressure both in his church and from his government because of a public stand on human rights issues. This has never been made public but the General Secretary cabled the government of the WCC's concern with the safety and rights of a "brother", a respected Christian leader from a neighbouring nation was asked to visit and "counsel" with the church authorities. The person involved was assisted to attend a conference outside the country. When he returned, the situation was much less tense.

CCIA Director Ninan Koshy believes that the WCC has to be selective in the issues it addresses. An "ecclesiastical running commentary" on world affairs is not necessary or desirable. He is also convinced that "what may be called the political witness of the WCC is significant only if the churches in their own situation are witnessing also".

The WCC comes under considerable criticism for its public reticence to criticize governments in Eastern Europe, especially the Soviet Union. One example comes from the *New Republic,* a once progressive magazine voice in the US now turned cold warrior; "Predicting who will be condemned by the WCC is easy. It has nothing to do with the relative level of violation of human rights, as documented, for example, by Amnesty International. A practically infallible predictor of who will be singled out by the WCC is a country's ideological affinity with the US."

42

But the problem is that the WCC has to ask what is best for the mission of the churches in those countries. That is a responsibility it has to live with every day.

After a fairly heated debate on repression and human rights violations in various parts of the world, the CWME Melbourne conference addressed the issue like this:

> Some countries and people we dare not identify for the simple reason that such a specific public identification by the conference may endanger the position — even the lives — of many of our brothers and sisters, some of whom are participating in this conference. We therefore confess our inability to be as prophetic as we ought to be as that may, in some instances, entail imposing martyrdom on our fellow believers in those countries — something we dare not do from a safe distance.

Communication Director John Bluck (New Zealand) wrote in *One World* (November 1980) about the issue. The WCC has six member churches in the Soviet Union — three Orthodox, two Lutheran and the Union of Evangelical Christian Baptists. "And the WCC is answerable to those churches for what it says and does — not just in terms of letters and meetings, but lives, properties and, above all, the very witness of the church itself."

Bluck's comment came as part of an introduction to the public release of a letter to Metropolitan Juvenaly, head of the Department of External Church Relations in the Moscow Patriarchate of the Russian Orthodox Church, detailing the extensive private correspondence concerning the arrests and sentencing of a number of priests and lay people and asking that the continued concern of the world church be conveyed to the proper authorities. The letter indicates considerable unpublicized expressions of concern. It says, at one point:

> ...we have consistently refrained from entering into public debate regarding such cases, even when member churches outside the USSR have urged us to do so, since we wish to preserve a sober and careful approach that respects the complexity and particular character of the context in which your church, with its millions of believers, as well as other Christian communities in your country, makes its witness. This pattern of consultation and reflection also expresses the nature of our relationship with all our member churches.

It should be noted that public silence is maintained in many other situations where the church might be put in jeopardy. Iran is one (although the General Secretary made two private appeals on behalf of the US hostages). The East Timor situation has been quietly addressed because the Indonesian church lives within a dominant Muslim culture.

The problem with the criticism made by the American magazine, and often directed at the WCC, is that it sees the world only in East-West terms. But the Council is a world body with churches from the east and the west, the north and the south, the rich and the poor, first, second, third, and fourth "worlds". The Western media widely reported the 1981 decision of the Salvation Army to withdraw its membership from the WCC because it felt the Council had become too political (the PCR Zimbabwe grant was its key objection) and because it had problems with the growing agreement on the sacraments. What was not reported was a demonstration by the Salvation Army in Zimbabwe protesting the world body's decision.

No-one ever promised an easy search for a just, participatory and sustainable society.

Commission on Inter-Church Aid, Refugee and World Service

A process of sharing

Kampuchea is one of the gravest human tragedies of our time. Mention the Sahel and many would think of the most desperate economic problems of any region in the world.

In both these situations the world's churches, through the WCC's Commission on Inter-Church Aid, Refugee and World Service (CICARWS), have been actively involved.

Prolonged drought since the late 1960s has devastated the semi-arid region of the Sahara known as the Sahel. The area stretches from Senegal on the west to parts of Ethiopia in the east and includes Cape Verde, Chad, Gambia, Mali, Mauritania, Niger and Upper Volta. Mass migration has added to the suffering from the shattered agricultural system and the death by starvation of thousands of people.

From the beginning of the crisis the churches of the world have been involved in relief aid and refugee assistance. In recent years they have done this together in the programme of solidarity for development in the Sahel. This is a long-term project with two priorities: food production and the training of rural development agents. Since 1974 an ecumenical team (averaging four members) has been based in Ouagadougou, Upper Volta, working together with 24 Sahelian counterparts.

In spite of built-in difficulties, the programme supports the participation of people at village level in the decision-making process that determines what is to be done to make their community more sustainable.

In 1978, the WCC through CICARWS committed itself to continue a ten-year programme in the area. This is to be reviewed in 1983. The programme asks the world church to supply $2 million a year to make this long-range effort, a considerable asking at a time when the Sahel is no longer receiving headlines as the restless media move on to other stories.

In Kampuchea, CICARWS, working with the Christian Conference of Asia (CCA) inside the country, and the Church of Christ in Thailand on the border between the two countries, has channelled over $15 million in emergency assistance to the Khmer people. This assistance has taken as its main concerns agriculture and medical help, and has been concentrated in the province of Siem Reap (site of the great Angkor Wat ruins).

When it appeared that the worst crisis was over, a series of natural disasters — drought and floods — set back the rebuilding efforts of this small nation of giant suffering. In answer to this CICARWS and the CCA brought in more rice seed, fungicide, vegetable seed, and superphosphates. Together, the churches of the world committed $3.5 million more in 1981 to help the Kampuchean people.

This Buddhist nation had a small Khmer Evangelical Church before the cataclysm of the 1970s. Three pastors survived, only one of whom now remains within Kampuchea itself. Nevertheless, church meetings began to take place in homes — the church buildings had been destroyed or were being used by the government. When it appeared that a new constitution being proposed guaranteed freedom of belief but not of public worship, the WCC/CCA staff made interventions on the church's behalf. At Christmas 1981, permission was granted to hold services on 24 and 25 December.

In the Sahels and Kampucheas of the world, the churches express their concern and solidarity through CICARWS, which emerged from the interchurch aid work that began in Europe immediately after World War II, when the WCC itself was in the process of formation. It was intended to exemplify a process of mutual aid — two or more churches helping each other — not a one-sided action where the rich or strong partner helps the poor and weak. It was seen as a process of sharing.

Service for justice

It is in the nature of CICARWS that it should be an enabler, assisting, coordinating and stimulating the churches in their desire to serve one another. In carrying out this task CICARWS is the representative of the churches acting together, and its own identity is not always obvious.

Mr Jean Fischer (Switzerland), who directs the almost 50 staff — some 25 per cent of the Council's programme staff work for CICARWS — and who succeeded Ms Muriel Webb (USA) after her untimely death in 1977, affirms that CICARWS is never alone.

> We have a mandate to respond to initiatives from member churches that find themselves in situations of difficulty or need or want. We communicate such appeals to all, asking for expressions of solidarity. Then some churches respond, others do not; some respond to some situations, others to other situations. We are permanently involved in one part of the world or another. It is not of our choice. We don't decide our programmes. We are here serving the churches as they live and witness in all kinds of difficult situations.

Fischer says that the involvement in the Sahel and Kampuchea is in fact not typical of the usual way CICARWS works, because no local member churches are present in these areas. The more usual approach is for CICARWS to respond to a call from a member church which has decided what needs to be done in a situation of crisis. What this church or council sees as its mission in its context is communicated by CICARWS to the other churches who respond in the way they can to the invitation to be in partnership.

A wide spectrum

CICARWS makes several divisions of its task. An emergencies office monitors earthquakes, floods, fires, civil wars and other upheavals, and shares the information and appeals for assistance with concerned churches and agencies which are ready to express their compassion with the victims of disasters. Among the emergency appeals in 1979, to take one year: victims of the Columbian earthquakes, those trapped by the East Timor conflict, homeless flood victims in Egypt, and Afghan refugees in Pakistan.

Material aid works closely with "emergencies" to coordinate the acquisition of materials for WCC-supported programmes. If goods are purchased, this is done if at all possible in the country where the programme is located or in a neighbouring state. In 1979, again, it helped provide agricultural, industrial and educational equipment for Guinea-Bissau, and put the Burma Council of Churches in touch with the Intermediate Technology Development Group (UK) to locate appropriate methods for making bricks and simple agricultural machinery.

46

Diakonia (service) promotes relationships and exchanges between deaconesses, deacons and lay social workers of all traditions, to make it possible for them to develop supportive relationships with each other. Together with the Swiss interchurch agency HEKS, it maintains a retreat centre in Switzerland for their use. Support for the International Year of Disabled Persons was provided by this office.

CICARWS also has an office concerned with *ecumenical personnel exchange*. Here skilled personnel are recruited for church needs, emergency situations, short- and long-term voluntary service, and team visitations among churches. From 1980 the "ecumenical sharing of personnel" emphasis, shared with CWME, has become part of this task. The work here is to place individuals from one church with another across geographical boundaries, a shift from the West to East movement (rich to poor, critics would say) of so much of missionary history.

CICARWS also has seven regional "desks" responsible for monitoring what is going on in the churches around the world. The task of these "area secretaries", as they are called, is to assist churches and ecumenical organizations to witness together through their pastoral, evangelistic, educational and social programmes. The staff members are administratively responsible for the hundreds of projects in all parts of the world which are supported through what is called the Project List. The 1980 listing of projects totalled almost $60 million and testifies to a substantial expression of mutual concern. Even so, because of historic, national and denominational relationships, this sum represents only about ten per cent of the giving and receiving of funds by churches within the WCC fellowship.

With the development in certain places of a country-wide programme (where all the WCC-related churches in a single country draw up a total programme), and the screening by regional committees, the determination of how the money will be used by the recipients has been greatly improved.

Since Paul gathered relief funds for the needy in Jerusalem (Rom. 15:25-26), the church has been a place of sharing. A significant part of the world Christian community has in recent years used the WCC as its vehicle to share in this way.

A review of the project system published in 1979 was widely circulated among WCC member churches. It emphasized that real sharing of ecumenical resources implied the interaction of human and financial, material and spiritual resources at all levels within the ecumenical movement.

Ideas from both this study and subsequent meetings are now being implemented under a study programme on the *Ecumenical Sharing of Resources* (ESR). The new "instrument" for sharing, replacing the old project list, tries to pick up many of the ideas expressed on the subject over the years.

An interesting inquiry into the issue is presented by Tracy Early in *Simply Sharing* (1980). The idea is obviously important and central to authentic Christian relations, one with another. But it is also difficult, bucking the current trends in fund-raising and church finance.

The Central Committee commended the study and implementation of the ideas and recommended that the publication *Empty Hands: an Agenda for the Churches* be used in the continuing enquiry. It offers the vision. Here are excerpts.

> Our wealth takes many forms. Every church, rich or poor, needs to recognize the greatness of its wealth in being the people of God. In the sharing of people, of our ways of proclaiming the gospel, our forms of worship, our insights into being human, we mutually enrich one another and build up one another in the fullness of Christ. It is in our "poverty" that we are open to receive from one another.
>
> Also every church must re-evaluate those other resources entrusted to it — its financial resources, its lands, its buildings, its investments — according to the criteria of the purpose of God's sharing. Both churches considering themselves rich and those considering themselves poor must face the fact that their fundamental sharing must not be simply with each other but with the world in all its needs and agony.
>
> ESR is also a perspective from which to view other ecumenical issues and other WCC concerns and programmes. It provides a renewed understanding of interchurch aid, a challenge to the churches in their relationships with one another and their use of institutional power, an expression of solidarity with the poor and the racially oppressed. It underlies the discussions on church union, the dialogue with other faiths and ideologies, people's participation in development. It is fundamental to the search for a new international economic order and a just, participatory and sustainable society.

The *Ecumenical Church Loan Fund* (ECLOF) is yet another function of CICARWS. Wishing to create self-reliance and confidence through making loans rather than grants, ECLOF has loaned more than $1 million a year since Nairobi to churches, agencies and other groups to finance projects which they have made their priority. Originally set up to help in the rebuilding of churches and church institutions after World War II, it still does this, but has expanded into development projects. It operates through a system of 51 national ECLOF committees.

The CICARWS *refugee service* helps churches and agencies to become involved in alleviating the plight of the world's millions of refugees. Through a network of churches, ecumenical agencies and international organizations, the rights of refugees are defended in such areas as asylum, material assistance and a place to build a future. In doing this, it joins in the WCC's work in promoting conditions which will no longer produce refugees and will allow those who have left to return home. This work is now carried on in 51 countries. The refugee service also works closely with intergovernmental organizations such as the UN High Commissioner for Refugees and with ecumenically-related agencies like the World YWCA. Financial, technical, coordinating and information-sharing assistance is provided. It also assists with the resettlement of refugees. Between 1978-1980 it helped to resettle about 75,000 refugees.

In the midst of this operational momentum — the dramatic increase in funds dispersed through CICARWS since Nairobi is a testimony to its work — CICARWS also performs an analytical function on behalf of the churches. One example is a document called "The Churches and the World Refugee Crisis" prepared in 1981. It begins: "A world refugee disaster of unprecedented proportions is fast developing, a cumulative nightmare for many millions of men, women and children forced to flee their homes."

Another office now under the CICARWS banner is that of the *Migration Secretariat*. Migrants are different from refugees, although both share "uprootedness". The work within the WCC has always had a relationship between the two but there are clear differences. Refugees move under internationally recognized conventions which clearly define their status. International agencies coordinate their work on refugees, the churches give it high priority, and the response to refugees rests, in part, on the compassionate, moral and legal international responsibilities of states. No conventions apply to migrant labourers, no international coordination takes place; their issue is primarily economic.

In following up the Nairobi call for the churches to "defend and promote the rights of migrant workers" the secretariat worked to support the churches in seeing a role of greater advocacy with migrants to supplement their pastoral role, to be directly involved with migrants and their issues, and to make certain that the migration issue became an integral concern of other programmes of the WCC, such as racism, transnationals, human rights and urban mission.

Another example of CICARWS's analytic function was a study of "the use and abuse of food aid in the fight against world hunger". Writer Jonathan Fryer produced *Food for Thought*, discussing some of the complexities of the food issue, and warns the churches which, "in their desire to assist all those who are hungry, might be tempted to use the easy limited reply: food aid".

The justice issues, the causes that lie behind human suffering, have played an increasing role in the deliberations of those involved in interchurch aid. Fischer said, in his director's address at the June 1981 meeting of the Commission:

> It is generally held that the institution of diakonia (Acts 6), with the appointment of the first seven deacons, was intended to relieve the apostles of material tasks and leave them free to devote themselves to the preaching of the word. However, at the very beginning of the affair there was an injustice, an instance of discrimination: "... widows were being overlooked in the daily distribution". It was to redress this injustice that a number of Hellenists, members of an oppressed minority, were appointed to wait at table: as a measure to guard against injustice and marginalization.
>
> When we look at our world and see all the men and women who are constantly overlooked in the daily distribution... *Our diakonia must aim to reestablish justice*, not to distribute the left-overs to those who are neglected, discriminated against, marginalized.
>
> To do this, our diaconal service must actively oppose the forces which are seeking to destroy life; it cannot make do with bringing solace and aid to people who have already been struck down and broken by those forces. Its role is preventive as much as curative.

Commission on the Churches' Participation in Development

The development debate

The Methodist Church of Bolivia is a spiritually rich church of materially poor people. It is made up primarily of Aymaras, the indigenous people whose ancestors ruled the Kollasuyo Empire before the Spanish *conquistadores* came to the High Andes in the 16th century. As with other so-called Indian communities of Latin America, the Aymaras suffered grievously from the colonial intrusions: they were enslaved, compelled to do forced labour, saw their families and communities destroyed.

Resistance against the outside power and, later, against those who assumed political control after independence, was sustained but futile. In some cases the churches helped the Aymaras paternalistically, but it was an institution of *gringos,* white people, representing little good news.

In the late 19th century, the Methodist Church sent missionaries to the Aymara communities of the Bolivian coast of the Titicaca Lake. Over time, the Aymaras became the majority of the Bolivian Methodist community. They began to assume leadership — a major step came when the first Aymara bishop to head the church was named — and the church's involvement in such programmes as health care was planned and carried out by the Aymaras themselves.

As one report puts it:

> Working together with a "Council of Amantas" (wise people), the Methodist Church in Bolivia is becoming an institution of the indigenous people in that country.... The effort towards a church of the Indians is an expression of the search for a church of the poor.... The message of the liberating gospel of Jesus Christ has gained a deeper meaning; it is no longer a manifestation of paternalism from the church, but rather a proclamation which helps them to understand better how to reaffirm their deep convictions and values.

The development debate revolves around one fact. The gap between the rich and the poor grows wider each year. The earlier optimism about foreign aid and good will overcoming the stark division of the world's people has long since congealed into pessimism bordering on despair. This presents a tremendous challenge to the churches. In late 1981 a hostile US television interviewer tried to entangle Philip Potter into a simplistic critique of the US economic system. Potter replied:

> We do challenge, as Christians, *any* system which brings about a situation, such as we have today, where two-thirds of humanity are in dire need while one-third enjoys two-thirds of the wealth of the world. This is intolerable for Christians.

The church has always been concerned about development, although the term is relatively new. In the Mediterranean the mission of the early church and later of the monks in Europe "laid the foundations of a more widely-based economic and social life", stated an editorial in the *International Review of Mission* in 1969. "Worship and work, proclamation and service, were integral to those who saw themselves continuing the mission of Christ who came that men might have life and have it more abundantly."

The missionary movement of the past two hundred years from Europe and North America brought change to the world, not least in a new emphasis on human dignity demonstrated, in part, by establishing hospitals, schools and centres for orphans and the elderly. But the past two decades have brought an increasing awareness of the social and structural entrapment that underlay what the French call "maldevelopment". And this critique of colonialism and neo-colonialism also called into question relationships enjoyed by many of the churches' missionary enterprises.

Development was not a neutral matter, a sharing of money and resources without any awareness of the distortions in the social and political structures. This was clear to the churches related to the WCC by the time of the 1968 Uppsala Assembly. The First Development Decade did not achieve a great deal, and the plight of the world's poor demanded response. The Uppsala Assembly warned that "to be complacent in the face of the world's need is to be guilty of practical heresy".

Developing a strategy

The WCC was asked by the Assembly to aid the churches in their work on development (now called self-development in some churches). A world consultation on Ecumenical Assistance to Development Projects was held in 1970 from which came the creation of the Commission on the Churches' Participation in Development (CCPD). The consultation provided an understanding of development that linked three objectives: justice, self-reliance and economic growth.

An ecumenical development fund (EDF) was established to make money available in situations where groups — which set their own priorities — are involved in work towards "justice and self-reliance".

The major instrument for fund-raising was the "2% appeal", which had been suggested at Uppsala, whereby churches were asked to set aside at least 2% of their annual income for development projects at home and abroad (the suggestion was that 25% be used at home for development education, 75% abroad, either bilaterally or through EDF). The appeal was not just to raise funds but to create an educational debate about sharing resources.

Dr Julio de Santa Ana (Uruguay), Director of CCPD since the retirement of C.I. Itty (India), says that from the beginning CCPD was aware that "development is not something you can do from a central office".

CCPD began by exploring how it could assist groups already involved in the "struggle" and at the same time help churches in the rich world move towards an understanding of what solidarity with the poor entailed. In the early years CCPD worked with a few selected groups to gain greater experience and understanding, linking Western churches in "counterpart" relationships.

This fed into the Nairobi Assembly which reiterated that the development process should be understood as liberating, aimed at justice, self-reliance and economic growth (i.e. just, participatory and sustainable). Essentially it is

> a people's struggle in which the poor and the oppressed are and should be the active agents and immediate beneficiaries. Seen in this perspective the role of the churches and the WCC is to support the struggle of the poor and the oppressed towards justice and self-reliance.

Shortly after Nairobi the full CCPD met and said that ecumenical development work should assist "churches and their constituency to manifest in their theological outlook, styles of life and organizational structures their solidarity with the struggle of the poor and the oppressed".

This understanding required a broader strategy. "You cannot talk about the churches' participation in development in Africa or Asia or the Middle East, or even development education activities in the affluent countries, without first linking groups and churches in the same region," says Santa Ana.

CCPD began to be involved with a larger number of groups. It related, with varying degrees of success, to regional networks — in some cases related to regional councils of churches — which define their priorities from their own situation. Then they ask CCPD to help provide support or find services. If a formal relationship develops, CCPD does its best to supply those funds or services. (Some Western governments, which believe the churches can provide assistance better than they can, have desired to channel some of their aid through the churches.) But the group determines finally how it will use the help. This reduces dependence, supports self-reliance, and allows flexibility. If, for example, a government changes, in some countries a project might no longer be allowed. But if the relationship is with a self-defined group of people, it can shift its priorities. CCPD has thus worked towards the creation of networks devoted to development as now defined: justice, self-reliance and economic growth, on the basis of people's participation.

A second way it has worked is to participate in the theological action and reflection on the meaning of the church's option for the poor, to use the phrase of the Catholic bishops at Puebla. For historical reasons, such an option does not seem to obtain in the lives of many churches which too often have been either openly allied with the rich or isolated from the debate. But some examples do exist: the Methodist Church in Bolivia, described at the beginning of this section; the amazing combination of worship and social action of the base communities of Brazil and other parts of Latin America, which have challenged and revitalized the church, primarily Roman Catholic but also Protestant; some sectors of the church in the Philippines and Korea; at times in Ethiopia. What they illustrate is how true mission and true development can go together. A church, in either poor or rich countries, which has hospitals or schools which serve only the elites, for example, will find that it has to explain why it is not anti-development.

Areas of involvement

To assist the churches in thinking through these issues, CCPD has been going through a theological and historical reflection activity over several years. This has produced three books which have received considerable attention. The first was an examination of the biblical and theological understanding of why the church must be in solidarity with the poor: *Good News for the Poor.*

The second book is *Separation Without Hope?,* a study where a number of experts examined the period from about 1750 to 1920 when the churches were unable to accept the challenge of the new working class.

The third, *Towards a Church of the Poor,* is a discussion of what is happening with those churches which have taken a clear option for the poor. All three studies are brought together in brief popular format, *Towards a Church in Solidarity with the Poor.*

It seems quite likely that this understanding of solidarity with the poor will be the most important "learning" of the CCPD experience in the first 12 years of its life. CCPD began with concern about the inadequacy of the responses to world poverty. It has moved to a challenge of the self-understanding of the churches about their mission. CWME through its work in the past few years on the nature of authentic mission and evangelism has also identified the presence of the poor as its greatest concern. (Together they may well be the most substantial advancement in the search for a just, participatory and sustainable society.)

CCPD shares some of its "findings" directly with other departments of the Council. It joins Church and Society in wondering how the third world will ever "participate" in the decisions about the technology which is being imposed. The Christian Medical Commission and CCPD agree with where priorities should be placed on health care. CCPD often finds some of its best examples in the work of Urban Rural Mission groups around the world. CCIA and CCPD agree that the arms race destroys development as much as any single factor.

CCPD has also been the coordinator of an advisory group on economic matters reaching for an economic vision that might undergird the JPSS. The findings of the first three hearings are contained in *Ecumenism and a New World Order: the Failure of the 1970s and the Challenges of the 1980s.*

In 1982 CCPD will sponsor a meeting on the search for justice in socialist societies, organized by its study secretary, Prof. Nikolai Zabolotski (USSR). Held in the Soviet Union, it will bring together both Eastern and Oriental Orthodox churches. It is an opportunity for them to discuss development and justice issues in their own language and context rather than in the Western Protestant style of much of the discussion so far.

CCPD is also engaged in development education, seeking ways to assist churches in keeping these issues in the forefront of their concern. Earlier, development education was seen primarily as sharing information. Now it is more and more understood to be involvement. One way to encourage that is the CCPD attempt to link first and third world churches in common concerns. Understanding the linkages among military spending, the struggle for human rights, and the demands for justice is one example of an educational issue that cuts across all the "worlds".

Santa Ana believes that development education — CCPD shares some of the experiences in an irregular series of dossiers — should also be frank about the difficulties of participating in real development: the limitations of what can be done, the complexity of acting, the difficulty of true solidarity, the forces opposed.

Certainly, CCPD's experience with the "2%" appeal" is sobering. Very few churches have responded to the call from the Uppsala Assembly. At one point CCPD hoped to raise $10 million annually to use with its counterpart groups. In its first 11 years it was able to distribute $21 million and now budgets slightly less than $3 million a year, not all of that by any means from the "2%" appeal".

Nor has the appeal engaged the churches in the kind of educational debate that CCPD hoped for, a kind on which the Dutch Reformed Church reported positively in 1980. The synod "appeals" to the congregations to set aside the 2% and it does keep 25% of that for development education in the Netherlands. The synod reported:

The greatest temptation at the moment is the desire to make the 2% rule no longer an item on the budget of the congregation but an appeal to the personal purse of the church members. Does this make any difference? First, it undoubtedly would bring in more money. But, second, it cuts out the conflict in the congregation. And that is, besides the financial anxiety, the main reason why it is proposed. And that is also the most important reason why the change should not happen. If the synod in 1970 had chosen this solution, the educational effect of the 2% rule would not have been a fraction of what it is now.

What it means to be the church in solidarity with the poor, what it means for churches who have not even tried to be in solidarity with the poor to make some steps in the process, will be told in the stories of congregations and base communities and worshipping communities around the world. But in a clergy conference in Zimbabwe in late 1980, the Rev. Canaan Banana, now president of Zimbabwe, issued the challenge for the church there. Many of the denominations, he said, had not only not opposed the racism and oppression against which the liberation struggle had been fought, they also discriminated in accommodations, salaries and other ways within their own structures. Because of such shortcomings, "people were progressively losing faith in the church... and its ability to communicate the whole gospel to the whole person".

The mission of the church should be to announce to the poor the good news of a society that is really free, really equal, really loving; a society in which power must be put at the service of the people and a society in which wealth is equitably shared.... The challenge is for the church to work tirelessly for the liquidation of social and economic systems that cause people to be naked, hungry and neglected, so that all human beings are valued in their dignity as the images of God.... It must try to abandon privileged positions in the centres of domination and become rooted in the lives of the poor. It must promote a wider and deeper fellowship.

The WCC works in several ways on the development issue; indeed, CCPD was created in part because several sub-units were involved, and CCPD was to give development a central focus. One interesting new approach since 1975 has been the Ecumenical Development Cooperative Society (EDCS), sometimes called an ecumenical or poor person's World Bank. CCPD, if not quite the parent, is at least the midwife of EDCS.

EDCS makes higher risk but smaller loans than the World Bank or the other international financial institutions. Investment capital from the churches and their agencies is made available in long-term low-interest loans to programmes designed to meet the needs of the poor.

EDCS, directed by Adrian Wijemanne, a Sri Lankan businessman who also directed ECLOF, says its purpose is to be a model for action in development cooperation. After seven years EDCS had 150 member subscribers, assets of $5 million, had loaned four of the five million, and appears to be catching on, in spite of scepticism in banking (and some church) circles.

For sure, it has led some churches with investment funds to educate themselves on what should be done with their money. In the US financial officers are required to adhere to the "prudent man rule" while investing funds, which means with attention to safety of investments and maximum return. The churches have begun talking about the "gospel person" response and one corporate lawyer seems to say this can be done. "An investment to promote the organization's corporate purposes must be viewed in the light that... any potential loss involved in the assumption of a risk higher than normal should be considered as equivalent to an expenditure for the corporate purpose."

Which is to be interpreted: investing money that helps the poor is part of the church's purpose.

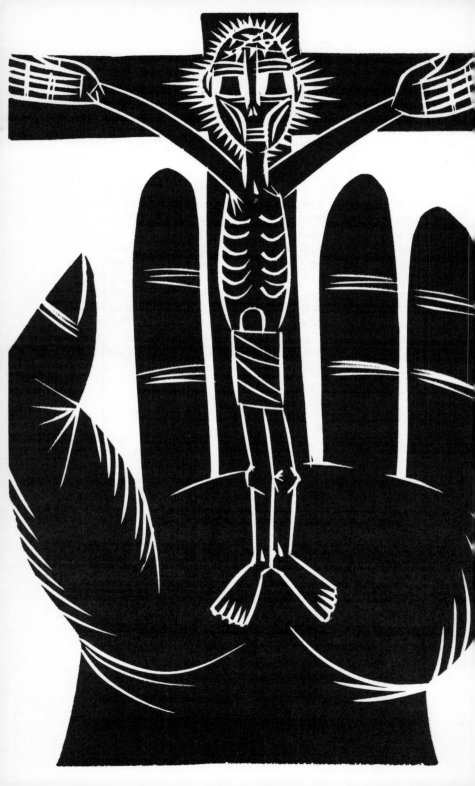

CHAPTER 3

THE UNITY OF THE CHURCH
AND ITS RELATION
TO THE UNITY OF HUMANKIND

Faith and Order

To proclaim the oneness of the church

The most divisive and painful moment at the Nairobi Assembly, wrote Dr Robert McAfee Brown, who gave the keynote address, came during the closing eucharist, which should have been the high point.

> (In Nairobi) the service was flawed. Every single one of the twenty or so celebrants was male, and among the communicants a significant number could not, for theological reasons, receive the elements. Both realities were shattering: I had expected the second but not the first, and their juxtaposition made me realize how far we still have to go.

Brown, who was writing in *Christianity and Crisis* magazine, said that the most powerful moments came during those times when the Lord's prayer was offered with participants using their own language.

> For at that moment, as at no other, the delegates are truly one. The unity is not uniformity, for differences of language are acknowledged, but it is deep, for it is the *same* prayer being said together by *all*.

It comes as a shock to many new to WCC assemblies that not all members can participate in a common eucharist. Nor do all member churches agree that the ordination and baptism practised by others are valid. These differences reflect the many ways in which the Council is still in the act of becoming.

The unity of the church has long been disturbed by doctrinal disagreements. But, and this has been increasingly recognized over the past ten years, division is created as well by the race, sex and class separations that also divide the human community.

One of the most significant occurrences in the period since Nairobi has been the "convergence" (a very popular ecumenical word these days in several areas) among theologians on the thinking and practice of baptism, eucharist and ministry. Equally important has been the continuing extension of the understanding of unity to include more than doctrinal questions.

Within the WCC the task of the sub-unit on Faith and Order (F&O) has been to hold before the churches the goal of visible unity in Christ. Again, it does not have the sole responsibility, because all of WCC is an expression of the churches striving for unity. The mandate of F&O appears both in its by-laws and in the WCC's constitution as one of its "functions and purposes":

> to proclaim the oneness of the church of Jesus Christ and to call the churches to the goal of visible unity in one faith and one eucharistic fellowship, expressed in worship and common life in Christ, in order that the world might believe.

In 1977 the churches celebrated the 50th anniversary of the First World Conference on Faith and Order, that special moment when the churches broke the silence of centuries to talk openly with one another about the doctrinal issues which separated them.

The ecumenical expression had come a long way since that Lausanne (Switzerland) gathering. Churches all over the world are in communion with one another in ways unthinkable at the beginning of the century. Dr Lukas Vischer (Switzerland), who left the Council in 1979 after almost two decades of staff association with F&O, reflected then on "just how profoundly relations between the churches have changed in the course of a few decades. New forms of common witness and new forms of common life continue their pioneering service."

But he also pointed out a paradox: in spite of all that has occurred divisions persist intact and, if anything, particularist currents run more strongly than ever. "It is as if, after years of strenuous endeavour on behalf of the common witness of Christians, a certain fatigue has set in. The more immediate circle of unity is preferred to the wider fellowship."

Over the decades each church has approached talks with other churches from its own set of presuppositions. The WCC, although brought into being to seek church unity, cannot take sides. Its role has been to challenge and support the dialogue between and among the churches on the question of unity.

To many, the visible unity of the church has meant organic union among churches, an occurrence that has inspired the whole fellowship many times — when it occurred in the Church of South India, the Uniting Church of Australia, the Evangelische Kirche der Union (FRG) and other instances. Perhaps 35 such conversations are seriously under way now.

At Nairobi the churches agreed upon an understanding of unity, called "unity in conciliar fellowship". If the representatives of the churches could come together in a full sharing of worship and confession of the faith, this too would be a sign of "visible unity". Conciliar fellowship is not different from full organic unity; it is an elaboration of it. The work of F&O during the period has been for the "visible unity of the church as a eucharistic and conciliar fellowship".

Some worried that this new understanding might confuse, and undercut the concern for organic church unions; others felt it did not permit sufficient diversity in the church. But without question it has stimulated various partners, ecumenical groups, churches, and Christian world communions to think again about the nature and challenge of church unity.

Supporting its plenary commission, one of the few structures anywhere in the church where Roman Catholics, Orthodox, Anglican and Protestant members share full voting membership, F&O has three organizing principles for its work. All are prerequisites for visible unity.

First is the ability to profess together the apostolic faith today, the "faith" in Faith and Order. Second, an agreement on common ways of teaching and decision-making, the "order" in Faith and Order. Third involves working together to surmount the thorniest theological difficulties regarding the sacraments of baptism, eucharist and ministry, which have played such a prominent role in the separation of the churches.

Of the three, the theological convergence on the sacraments is by far the most advanced, and entered an unprecedented stage in 1982 after the F&O Commission held its triennial meeting in Lima, Peru.

Work in innumerable conferences and extensive research have gone on for the past fifty years to reach a measure of agreement on the most controversial aspects of the sacraments in order to come to some common ground. The theologians and church officials, who had worked for so long on these issues, reached considerable agreement before Nairobi. Their findings were shared with the member churches, some 150 of whom have made substantial response. Revised statements emerged to respond to the responses.

In 1982 this convergence material on baptism, eucharist, and ministry, co-authored by what Dr William Lazareth (USA), Director of F&O since 1980, calls "as broadly representative a spectrum of Christian thinking as has been organized in modern church history", goes to the churches for an official response. It is the first step of a process that is technically called "reception".

The material sent out includes the "Lima text" with its commentaries on reconciling statements. Also available will be a volume of theological and liturgical essays to explain how choices were made among alternative proposals, a lay study guide for classes and discussions, and other resources — liturgical, educational, and devotional — for use in local parishes and congregations.

The churches are asked to study and use these materials and, simultaneously, to make an official response to the text by 31 December 1984, concerning their faithfulness to scriptures and tradition, their ecumenical consequences for relations among the churches involved, and suggestions for relating this material to other aspects of the common expression of the apostolic faith today.

What this means is clear. The theologians have come to an agreement. Now it is up to the bishops to respond. Which is a shorthand way of saying the official structures of the churches must now consider what their own appointed specialists have achieved together. This new stage in the ecumenical journey will create some interesting challenges. Many Protestant churches do not have an apparatus for an official church response of this nature; the Orthodox and Roman Catholics do, but have not exercised it before on a document co-authored with people from outside their own church.

One example of what the form of this material looks like comes from the statement on ministry. This is chosen because it relates to the specific issue of the ordination of women to "the ministry of men and women in the church", about which considerable debate has already taken place within the churches in recent years.

The ministry of men and women in the church

Where Christ is present, human barriers are being broken. The church is called to convey to the world the image of a new humanity. There is in Christ no male or female (Gal. 3:28). Both women and men must discover together their contributions to the service of Christ in the church. The church must discover the ministry which can be provided by women as well as that which can be provided by men. A deeper understanding of the comprehensiveness of ministry which reflects the independence of men and women needs to be more widely manifested in the life of the church.

Though they agree on this need, the churches draw different conclusions as to the admission of women to the ordained ministry. An increasing number of churches have decided that there is no biblical or theological reason against ordaining women, and many of them have subsequently proceeded to do so. Yet many churches hold that the tradition of the church in this regard must not be changed.

62

Commentary

Those churches which practise the ordination of women do so because of their understanding of the gospel and of the ministry. It rests for them on the deeply held theological conviction that the ordained ministry of the church lacks fullness when it is limited to one sex. This theological conviction has been reinforced by their experience during the years in which they have included women in their ordained ministries. They have found that women's gifts are as wide and varied as men's and that their ministry is as fully blessed by the Holy Spirit as the ministry of men. None has found reason to reconsider its decision.

Those churches which do not practise the ordination of women consider that the force of nineteen centuries of tradition against the ordination of women must not be set aside. They believe that such a tradition cannot be dismissed as a lack of respect for the participation of women in the church. They believe that there are theological issues concerning the nature of humanity and concerning christology which lie at the heart of their convictions and understanding of the role of women in the church.

The discussion of these practical and theological questions within the various churches and Christian traditions should be complemented by joint study and reflection within the ecumenical fellowship of all churches.

This represents a considerable challenge for the churches. Lukas Vischer wrote in *One World* in 1977 that theologians have been falsely blamed for the lack of agreement on questions of unity. In fact "there is today more agreement than the churches are capable of absorbing. The historical reality of their confessional identity is too heavy to be moved. Unity cannot be achieved without considerable change on the part of the churches."

Most church divisions come from controversies of the fourth, sixteenth and eighteenth centuries. This convergence material is an attempt to reach back into the scriptures and creeds of the early undivided church so that participants can express their common Christian identity — the apostolic faith — rather than debate their subsequent histories.

To confess the faith together

The second dimension of F&O's work concerns an expanded "common expression of the apostolic faith today". If the churches are to live in unity, they must be able to convince one another that they share the same faith. The difficult issue has always been how and in what form to make this common confession. Many of those who came to Lausanne in 1927 expected to be able to make progress on this. They were disappointed. It has scarcely been attempted since. Now that theological convergence has been achieved on the disputed issues of the sacraments, F&O is incorporating that dialogue into a long-range study of how to confess all the essentials of the Christian faith together in our day.

According to Dr Lazareth this will not be an attempt to write a new creed or to create an ecumenical theology (the convergence texts on the sacraments are not a complete theology of the sacraments either). It is rather the limited attempt ecumenically to overcome those incompatible sectarian positions that prevent churches and people from communing with each other.

The process will not be easy but the experience with F&O's study of "Giving Account of the Hope" which began in 1971 and reached its culmination in 1978 encourages those involved.

Dr C.S. Song (Taiwan), who was the staff person responsible for the study, recalls that the intention was to reverse the usual method of F&O studies. The decision was made "to go to the people for their reflections and their contributions rather than to convene a group of theologians to come up with a statement. What happened was that study groups in various parts of the world reflected on the Christian faith within their own social, cultural, historical setting."

The response to what Lukas Vischer calls an attempt to work from below rather than above was surprising. "It was almost as if people had been waiting for such an invitation."

The widely varying contributions were collected and brought to Bangalore, India, for the 1978 triennial commission meeting (in the tradition that began in Lausanne in 1927) bringing together 160 representatives of various Christian traditions from more than fifty nations.

During the two-week session, several attempts failed at a common draft.

> But, to the amazement of all, when the final revised text was read on the last morning of the meeting, the commission members rose to their feet in spontaneous and prolonged applause! In spite of everything, a common account they could identify with had been produced. Everyone knew that for Christians of such diverse backgrounds to be able to speak of their hope with a common voice was a remarkable achievement.... the diversities evident in the lives and hopes of Christians are not smoothed over. Rather, the common account grows directly out of an encounter between them. That is its special significance. From that encounter has come a statement in which all together recognize the deepest ground of their common hope.

The brief ten-page statement is written in lively prose, not in the technical language of the scholar. Many local congregations and other church bodies have used it in their further reflections on "Living in Hope". The introduction catches the flavour:

> Everywhere songs of hope and longing are being sung. We have been able to listen to many of them in the accounts of hope which we have studied. There is a bewildering variety: from those who hunger for bread, justice and peace; those who long for freedom from religious or political persecution; those who hope for deliverance from infirmities of body and mind; those seeking a new community of women and men; those who search for cultural authenticity; those who hope for a responsible use of science and technology; those who evangelize and work for the spread of the gospel; those who labour for the visible unity of the churches. We have even become aware of intimations of hope from those who are silenced. In their silence itself is a word for those who can hear it. We have been listening to these voices because we ourselves are called to give an account of our hope. Always be prepared to make a defence to anyone who calls you to account for the hope that is in you (1 Pet. 3:15).

As the churches work on confessing the same apostolic faith today, mutual pressures will arise. Non-credal churches will be asked how they relate to classical creeds like the Nicene Creed, formulated by the ecumenical councils of the early church. They in turn will ask credal churches what these creeds really mean in today's world where the context and the challenges are very different. Such questions about official recognition and current exposition may expand the horizons sufficiently to allow movement towards a common confession of faith that would join the common agreement of the sacraments.

The third area in working towards unity stressed in F&O is the mutual acceptance of authoritative teaching bodies within the churches to receive what has been accomplished with baptism, eucharist and ministry and may happen with the common confession. How are the churches able to teach, speak and act together? As the common basis of belief grows, will incompatible structures prevent unity?

In some ways these inter-related issues of reception, mutual recognition and common witness have the potential to bring about the debate about the nature and forms of church and conciliar structure (ecclesiology) that was avoided in the creation of the WCC in 1948. At that time, in order to assure the membership of a wide variety of churches, WCC membership required only acceptance of the "basis", confessing the Lord Jesus Christ as God and Saviour. Since then, for thirty years churches have been breaking down walls of separation in proclaiming the gospel in word and deed together. A reappraisal of the developing meaning of a "fellowship of churches" is a pregnant possibility in ecumenical relations.

To witness to the unity of humankind

These developments in the work for the visible unity of the church, as they are reflected in united and uniting churches and the debate about conciliar fellowship, are related also to the renewal of the human community. "God so loved the *world*..." (John 3:16). Along with manifesting its unity in Christ, the church is to be united in order to witness to the renewal and unity of humankind.

The cleavages, moreover, between rich and poor, black and white, male and female, able and disabled are causes of disunity both in the world and in the churches. It is on these issues that F&O and many other segments of the WCC work closely together towards unity.

One brief example: disabled persons find themselves divided from full participation in the human and church community, by practice if not by conscious policy (although some churches do not ordain seriously disabled people).

The Nairobi assembly addressed the problem:

> A church which seeks to be truly united within itself and to move towards unity with others must be open to all; yet able-bodied church members, both by their attitudes and their emphasis on activism, marginalize and often exclude those with mental or physical disabilities.

The WCC made several contributions to the 1981 International Year of Disabled Persons. One was *Partners in Life: the Handicapped and the Church,* a book compiled by F&O.

Two other examples of disunity, racism and sexism, will be given more lengthy treatment as they have been approached by the WCC in the study on the Community of Women and Men in the Church and the Programme to Combat Racism.

F&O does other work, of course. It meets with Christian World Communions, is called as consultant for bilateral dialogues between churches, and in late 1981 convened the fourth consultation of United and Uniting Churches which issued a challenge to Christians around the world to renew their commitment to church unity.

F&O worked with PCR on a common venture, "Racism in Theology; Theology against Racism". F&O was asked to conduct the Bible studies at the 1980 ten-year stock-taking on the work of PCR and the churches on racism. William Lazareth, who did the studies, was asked about his thesis at the consultation.

If a church separates baptized Christians from holy communion for no other reason than the percentage of melanin in their skin, that raises the sociological issue of race relations to the theological level of idolatry. If, along with faith, I must bring race to appropriate God's undeserved grace, that is an issue of disorder in which Faith and Order is vitally concerned. We must protest in the name of God's word whenever and wherever a social practice is idolatrously ideologized by way of an heretical theology.

F&O, along with the Sub-unit on Renewal and Congregational Life, worked with the world bodies for the Methodists, Lutherans, Baptists, Reformed and Roman Catholics, to produce an ecumenical prayerbook called *For All God's People*. It offers a weekly description of a geographical group of churches and encourages intercessory prayer. The introduction says:

> Centuries of division have led to estrangements between the churches which are still far from overcome. But the walls of separation have begun to crumble. More and more we realize that, despite our differences, we form one family. Let us therefore offer regular prayers of intercession for *all* who call upon the name of Christ.

To do theology in context

Faith and Order has always been seen to be the place where theologians meet. Some of the best minds in the theological field have given of their time and energies over the years to help provide a theological basis for the ecumenical endeavour. F&O has always had a limited budget and that problem has only grown more difficult with recent financial difficulties. Lazareth believes this is one place where the sharing of resources has been real. "No amount of money could purchase the services freely given over the years by some of the best scholars in the world."

But it is also true that the style within the Council and within F&O is expanding. That is reflected in the "Giving Account of the Hope" and "Community of Women and Men" studies.

Philip Potter was asked about this.

> In the past decade a new emphasis has been placed on doing theology. Theology is not something ontological and eternal but is very earthy because it is the encounter of the Word of God with the words of people in the realities where they live. Anyone pretending to do universal theology is denying the incarnation. Paul's letters are very deeply affected by the places he's writing to and the situation of the people in Ephesus, Corinth, Thessalonica, etc. To impose on Paul one idea, justification by faith, is nonsense. In one place redemption, in another place reconciliation, is the theme. Some people want to write off James, others Revelation. But the biblical canon is a unity of faith. Can we do less?

At the 1980 world conference on the churches facing racism in the 1980s, different ways of doing theology were affirmed. Many of those who had come to the meeting had been involved in "contextual" theology, looking in depth at one's own context which then challenges one to a "theology in action, a living out of faith as Christians".

Doing theology from our context is important to stimulate us to respond in faith. The consultation report then said:

> But this is partial and does not deny the more comprehensive tradition of theological thought. Contextual theology is pluralist by its very method. Since specific historical and cultural contexts will yield only partial theological reflections, they will need to be correlated with each other within the worldwide church. This process of mutual learning and correction will yield a truly ecumenical vision.

What has been exciting to the WCC is that it has become one place where these many streams — liberation theology, feminist theology, black theology, theology of the people from Asia, new African thought, and more — have brought their "partial gospel" into interplay. It was indeed almost as if people were waiting for an invitation. Perhaps the leader was having to run to catch up with the people, in Gandhi's famous phrase.

Marie Assaad, Deputy General Secretary since 1980 and a member of the Egyptian Coptic Church, was asked whether she thought liberation theology was predominant. "I don't know what that means, really, because there are so many kinds of liberation theology. What I do know is that coming here from where I do, I realize for the first time how male dominated, how Western dominated and, if I may allow myself, how much German theology dominated, the whole theological enterprise really still is."

But theology is now being done all over the world, and that is a sign of hope.

The Community of Women and Men in the Church

A programme of worldwide study

If the decade of the 1960s brought a new understanding of the way both institutions and individuals display racial discrimination, consciously or unconsciously, the 1970s identified the ways in which women have been prevented from expressing their full humanity.

The past decade has witnessed a remarkable and worldwide expansion of the understanding of the roles and participation of women in society. How these issues have been addressed often reflects the society: what a woman in London cites as oppressive may differ sharply from a woman in Central America. But it is correct to say that in the early 1970s sexism as an issue joined racism on the ecumenical agenda.

Certainly the work of the Council has been affected. Philip Potter believes that "what emerged in this decade is a whole series of women's struggles which have challenged the presuppositions of our thinking in the same way the Latin Americans have challenged a lot of presuppositions of Western theology". Within the life of the church the basic fact is this: women make up a preponderance of those actively involved in the life of the church but have never played a commensurate role in the church's decision-making and leadership.

The unity of the church and the renewal of the human community demand a changed relationship between women and men.

In January 1982, the Lima meeting of the Faith and Order Commission received the final report of a study on the "Community of Women and Men in the Church". The study had brought women and men together in serious dialogue all across the globe. The process has been called a "breakthrough" and promises to echo in the churches for years to come. In the words of Philip Potter:

> The main thrust of this worldwide study, which has involved hundreds of groups of women and men, is first of all an exposé of our broken relationships through institutionalized male domination not only in societies but in the church. (The report asks us) to look afresh at received attitudes and interpretations of scripture as well as our entrenched practices in the light of God's design for humanity as a community of women and men.

How it began

The community study has its own history which helps place it within the ecumenical spectrum. Throughout the life of the ecumenical movement, women have played a key role. But in spite of a number of outstanding individuals one can name, it is a fact that in the representative meetings of the WCC, such as assemblies and the Central Commmittee, women are a small minority, and this reflects situations in most member churches. Even now women on the Council's programme staff are no more than 10 per cent.

In 1974 the sub-unit on Women in Church and Society organized a consultation in Berlin bringing together about 200 women to discuss "Sexism in the 70s". For most it was a new experience, an international meeting where women were not a minority. No seminar on theology had been planned — one participant said the planners thought theology had nothing to say to women — but one was organized and 23 women joined. It was a lively interchange among women, most of whom had studied theology but were now in other professions. Dr Constance Parvey, a Lutheran pastor in Boston, USA, was one of those in the seminar.

> It was out of this group that the idea behind the community study emerged. As we shared our own stories, we discovered that, though we were all serious and committed Christians, we were marginal to the church's institutional life. Most of our contributions to the life and thought of the church had come on our own initiatives and not because we have been involved in church structures.

Several of the women travelled a month later to Accra, Ghana, to the F&O Commission meeting, already discussing one aspect of the issue as part of its work on baptism, eucharist and ministry, and the unity of the church and human renewal. Later the Nairobi Assembly mandated the Council "to take up the task of mining the depths of this challenge and coming up with some new resources and paths for the church's future".

It took some time to determine where to place it in the Council's structure. The women wanted it related to the women's desk, where the constituency is, but they also wanted it to remain in F&O. Women already took the issue seriously. It was important that the churches take it seriously as well. It was finally located in F&O, as a joint project of the two sub-units.

Then the question arose of how to fund the study. Several women's organizations decided to withhold initial support because they felt it was the responsibility of the official member churches to provide the funds. They did not want this to be a study financed and supported only by women.

How it was carried out

Constance Parvey was asked to staff the study. When she arrived in 1978, she faced the question of how it was to be done. The tried and true way, within the churches and WCC past history, was to convene a group of experts to produce a consensus statement. But that did not seem appropriate for this task or for a time when F&O itself had begun involving churches and groups more broadly in its theological task, both through its process of working towards agreed statements and its "Giving Account of the Hope" study.

What Parvey did, with the help of her committee, was to design a study book appropriate to invite wide participation. After eight months of discussion with over 200 people in all parts of the world, a trial edition was used in the first regional consultation in Bangalore, just before the commission met which produced *Sharing in Hope*. The cross-cultural participation brought about a study book which called first for personal involvement rather than academic research.

With modification, the study guide was printed, a modest 3,000 copies. It caught on. An estimated 65,000 copies of the study book were reproduced, often at local initiative, in at least 13 languages, adapted to community situations and, most important, used by hundreds of groups. It took the staff by surprise. It took the churches by surprise.

The study questions, to be freely adapted, had three sections: personal and cultural, church teachings, and church structures. Four questions were to be kept in mind while discussing these: what is the present situation in your church, why are things the way they are, what is your vision for the community of women and men, and how can you move from where the church is to your vision of community?

Regional consultations, in Asia, Africa, Latin America, the Middle East, the USA and Europe, brought some of these threads together. Three specialized meetings — the "Ordination of Women in Ecumenical Perspective", the "Authority of Scripture in Light of New Experiences of Women", and "Theological Anthropology: Towards a Theology of Human Wholeness" — added to the rich resources which fed into the world consultation held in Sheffield, UK, in June 1981.

The Sheffield conference brought together women and men from 55 countries and 100 member churches. More than half the participants had been involved locally or regionally in the study. The full story will be told in a book to be published in 1982. One of those present at Sheffield described the meeting as celebrative rather than angry — a vivid, intense working together of women and men, on issues that have separated them. First and third world dialogue was as much a part of the discussion as was that between women and men. Concern for women, third world participants emphasized, cannot be valid without commitment to liberation from race and class oppression also.

The conference sent a number of recommendations to the Central Committee and others to specific units of the WCC. It called upon the WCC to "evaluate its own programme and procedure in regard to racism, sexism and classism". The recommendations of the study will be a part of the Vancouver Assembly in 1983.

Women in Church and Society

The study on the "Community of Women and Men in the Church" was a specific programme which has now been concluded. As the results of the study work their way in the churches, the sub-unit on Women in Church and Society continues to fulfill its mandate for advocacy and enablement of women.

The sub-unit, in one form or another, is as old as the Council itself. Its story through the years is vividly told in *A Voice for Women: the Women's Department of the World Council of Churches* by Susannah Herzel (1981). It is the story of how, "before men and women could discover a new level of relationship, women themselves needed to find and develop their own hidden voice".

The office is now headed by Bärbel von Wartenberg (FRG). She took over from long-term director Brigalia Bam in 1979, whose personality has left its imprint on the work of the department. As a black South African Ms Bam had painfully learned the importance of solidarity. Ms von Wartenberg is convinced that the most significant contribution made by the sub-unit through the years is that it has promoted a strong sense of solidarity among a large number of women from all over the world. It has through the years built a network of committed women. In turn the network, has strengthened their solidarity. They have been concerned over issues like peace, human rights and racism and how they affect women in particular. This concern often led to concrete action, as in the boycott of South African products or the protests against prostitution tourism organized by women in several countries. With the growing solidarity has come increased understanding between women of the first and third worlds.

Among the consultations organized by the sub-unit since Nairobi, four deserve special mention because in all four cases they broke new ground.

In September 1976 a consultation of Orthodox women was held in the Moldavian region of Romania. Its theme was the role of Orthodox women in the church and in society. For the first time a group of Orthodox women had come together to grapple with issues like family, education, witness and ecumenism, society and monasticism. Among the recommendations made by the consultation was one which urged "that the question of the ordination of women be studied in the light of the Orthodox tradition for more effective articulation of the Orthodox position in the ecumenical dialogue".

A consultation of church women executives met in Glion, Switzerland, in January 1977. There were 80 participants, the majority of them women who carried responsibility in their countries for work with Christian women. "But when you saw them together as a group", commented one of the participants, "their great diversity was clearly evident — differences in levels of responsibility, differences in the church structures and policies they represented, and differences in their individual theological perspectives. They had only two points in common: the fact that they were all women, and a live faith in Jesus Christ, supplemented by a desire to be his true disciples and determination to work out together what this implies."

The consultation took a close look at the lives women lead in the churches, in rural areas and under conditions of stress. It gave special attention to the whole issue of human rights and came up with strategies for action. The statement it issued listed specific violations of human rights — like the violation of the right to dissent, torture of political prisoners, secret trials of prisoners, violation of land rights, economic exploitation and the arbitrary censorship of the press. The participants pledged themselves to deepen their awareness and "to work towards the development of structures and systems which make possible just and humane societies".

"Women, Human Rights and Mission" was the theme of another consultation which was held in Venice in June 1979. There the participants reviewed those areas of women's lives where blatant violations of human rights continue to exist. "Those living under such conditions were invited to tell the facts of their situation, in the hope that exposure of these experiences would waken those who heard, not only to the recognition of the reality of specific violations of human rights, but to a new commitment of solidarity with all those voiceless women all over the world who suffer and a willingness to enter into their pain."

In July 1978, over 50 women theological students met at Cartigny, Switzerland, to talk about theology, ministry, spirituality, mission and theological education — and of course to share with one another their dreams for the future of the church. They were united in their experience of isolation and their anxiety to develop a theology that lives in the world of people, but they differed in their approaches to "feminism". "For so long limited to church pews, women envision a church structure that is horizontal — a mutually serving and supportive community built on the faith of all members of the congregation — rather than a church led from above."

The sub-unit's concern is not only with educated women or theologically trained women. Priscilla Padolina (Philippines) is secretary for women and rural development. Her work involves encouraging programmes of self-reliance for rural women, who are much more than a majority of women. Through a series of workshops at regional and national levels, rural women are enabled to identify the problems they face in their specific situations. Padolina also wants to strengthen their participation in churches and communities. "As the situation is now, women make up most of the world's food producers," she says. "Yet they are *least* included in the development process."

"The concerns of women", Nairobi had said, "must be consciously included in every aspect of the deliberations of the WCC." Increasingly the work of the sub-unit reflects this inclusiveness, and programmes are worked out in dialogue and cooperation with other sub-units. The office is working, for example, with the Programme to Combat Racism on a joint research and communication project on racism, and with the Christian Medical Commission on the meaning of health, healing and wholeness.

Programme to Combat Racism

It has been suggested that the growing claims by women on a role as partners in the life of the churches may become as explosive as the issue of race has been, not least because within all the churches women are a majority community. That remains to be seen. It is certain that the WCC's stands on racism have brought harsh reactions from church and non-church critics.

The reason is obvious, as Philip Potter points out. "In recent years our Programme to Combat Racism (PCR) has come under fire not because we denounce racism as sin. We have been doing that for over fifty years. Rather, it is because, through hard and patient study and research, through opening our eyes to the realities, we have exposed the whole anatomy of racial oppression and the ways in which people around the world, especially in the rich countries, have been involved concretely in maintaining racism."

Nothing has been a larger blight on the human community than racism. It was to help the churches, concerned about the unity of the church and its relation to the unity of the human community, that PCR was formed. And nothing has created more reaction to the work of the Council than the 12-year history of PCR. What it is and how it works will be described later. For now, a story.

Racism in Australia

For several weeks in June and July of 1981 the Australian media were dominated by reports about the conditions in which their

Aboriginal people live. The original inhabitants of the Australian continent for 40,000 years before the coming of the British colonists 200 years ago, they have dwindled to about 160,000 people (debate exists on the true number and whom to count), one per cent of Australia's population.

A recent national Aboriginal health survey points to their condition: life expectancy is 52 years, 20 below that of the Australian community at large; infant mortality is three times as high; trachoma, a blinding eye disease, is 15 times more common; in certain areas, they have the highest leprosy rate in the world. Only two per cent finish the ninth year of school, unemployment is 37 per cent, and only six lawyers and no doctors have been trained in the Aboriginal community.

The issue had been highlighted by the visit of a five-person WCC team who travelled more than 10,000 kilometres in 18 days within Australia at the invitation of the Australian Council of Churches (ACC). Their assignment: "To assess the situation of Aborigines, express solidarity with the Aboriginal people, consult with the churches and bring greater international attention to the situation of Aborigines, particularly in regard to land rights."

The team was composed of two members of the Central Committee, Pauline Webb, British Methodist and Director of Religious Programming for BBC World Service, and Bena-Silu, nuclear physicist and leader in the Kimbanguist Church of Zaire; two members of the PCR Commission, Elisabeth Adler, Director of the Evangelical Institute in East Berlin, and Quince Duncan, active Episcopalian and university lecturer in Costa Rica; and political scientist Anwar Barkat, former General Secretary of the Church of Christ in Pakistan and now Director of PCR, replacing Baldwin Sjollema (Netherlands) who departed in 1981 after long service to the WCC.

At the end of their visit, they issued a hard-hitting report, *Justice for Aboriginal Australians.* In an accompanying letter to the Aborigines, they thanked them for the warm welcome they received wherever they went and pledged to use all the means available to make their cause known across the world.

The report called the Aborigines the "invisible, unseen and unheard" people of Australia. And it suggested that "powerful multinational interests" have, with the states (which have considerable power in a federal system), deprived Aborigines of their rights.

The most explosive part of the report, for the general public, was about racism. The team was asked constantly if it thought Australia,

75

which only in recent years has modified a notorious "whites only" immigration policy, was a racist society. After offering, in the report, a definition of racism, the team found that "racism is entrenched in every aspect of Australian society".

The report accused the state governments of Queensland and West Australia, where the largest numbers of Aborigines live, of employing "hostile and racist ways to prevent Aborigines from gaining land or any measure of self-determination".

To which the Queensland premier (who refused to meet the team) replied, in language not unfamiliar in attacks on the WCC, that the PCR was formulated in Moscow and carried into the WCC by the KGB. Sir Charles Court, West Australian premier (who also refused to meet the team) called the report "a shameful collection of exaggerations, distortions, and self-contradictions".

The Canberra Times (in the federal capital) wrote editorially that it is not easy to be found wanting, especially after accommodating to a situation which "can fairly be described as unjust, inhumane, even despicable".

> (The WCC) report represents a watershed, an opportunity for a turning point, away from inaction and the national near-complacency of recent years.... Several leading politicians have already met some of its findings head on, as a challenge to be disputed and discounted. They are wrong; the findings are a challenge to be encountered with humility, not with angry denials or attempts at justification.

In a Gallup Poll conducted four weeks after the report appeared (the first printing of 2,000 sold out immediately; 5,000 more went almost as quickly) 53 per cent of those polled agreed that "racism is entrenched in every aspect of Australian society" (40 per cent disagreed), 53 per cent felt that the Aboriginal people on reserves should be given land rights and 50 per cent felt the governments were not doing enough for the Aborigines (18 per cent felt they were doing too much).

Ms Jean Skuse, General Secretary of Australian Council of Churches (the ACC is composed of Anglican, Church of Christ, Salvation Army, Society of Friends, Uniting Church in Australia and seven Orthodox communions), called the poll "a remarkable vindication of the integrity and accuracy of the WCC team's observations and findings".

The question of the Aborigines was also raised at the Commonwealth heads of government meeting convened in September in Australia. It was formally introduced by Prime Minister Indira

Gandhi of India and particular mention was made of the WCC report by Premier Efi of Western Samoa. He later told a press conference: "This meeting has given the WCC report publicity which will probably aid the cause of the Aborigines."

The WCC team visit made the impact it did in large part because the Australian churches created a receptive climate. The idea of inviting a team had grown directly out of the CWME Melbourne meeting in 1980 which heard, as part of its concern with the poor and the kingdom of God, directly from Aborigines about their situation. One month before the ACC had sponsored a meeting of the churches on racism as part of the process leading up to the PCR ten year world evaluation conference. It had faced head on the challenge of the Aborigines and was supportive of the assembly resolution that, among other things, a team be invited.

It was. The WCC Executive Committee accepted. The responsibility was given to the PCR.

In a foreword to the report, Skuse stated that the important question is:

> How will the Australian churches and the Australian community respond? One thing is clear; the Aboriginal people are looking to the church as perhaps the one remaining institution in Australian society to which they can turn for support.

A partial answer was not long in coming. Synods which met after the visit in 1981 made the report a topic of serious discussion. Several specific actions followed. The Uniting Church in Australia handed over properties worth about US$300,000 in an inner suburb of Sydney "as an unqualified gift to Aboriginal people". The resolution for the action referred to the request in the report which asked the churches to give land and money to Aborigines "as an act of reparation and reconciliation".

It rejected an approximately $12 million hotel/motel commercial project near central Alice Springs in favour of another proposal which will involve the "Aboriginal people".

Skuse responded:

> The quick and very positive response from so many church bodies around Australia has been most encouraging. The WCC team visit has had a tremendously beneficial effect on the life and witness of the Australian church and for this we give thanks to God.

This story, told at some length (and yet inadequate to its true richness), serves as an introduction to the highly visible, continuingly controversial Programme to Combat Racism. It is not a typical story because the tremendous media interest was more positive than usually greets PCR activities. It is also not typical of other WCC activities. The CWME Melbourne assembly, the largest and most diverse ecumenical gathering in Australian history, was greeted with almost total media silence.

Beginnings, functions

The "race problem" had been an ecumenical concern since the earliest days of the movement. But it was Uppsala which gave the clear call "to embark on a vigorous campaign against racism".

The WCC followed this by convening a consultation on racism in 1969. In a paper sent to the meeting, former General Secretary Visser 't Hooft told the group that "we have believed too much in persuasion by declarations and have not been sufficiently aware of the irrational factors of the situation" and that the real issue "is not whether Christians want inter-racial justice and equality, but whether they are willing to pay the price for it locally".

That meeting reaffirmed the right to resist tyranny which had been accepted (with principled disagreement from pacifists) since the Reformation. It urged that the WCC should be involved in a number of steps in the struggle against racism and "all else failing, the church and churches (should) support resistance movements, including revolutions, which are aimed at the elimination of political or economic tyranny which makes racism possible".

From the outset PCR, created by the 1969 Central Committee, has had three inter-related functions.

The first is *research and publications* on racism. A good deal of work has been done in this area on Australian Aborigines, the plight of Latin American Indians, the self-determination struggle of the Dene people in Canada, the immorality of the "bantustan" policy in South Africa. This work underlay policy statements of the Central Committee calling for a withdrawal of investments from South Africa (1972), an end to bank loans to the South African government and its agencies (1974), and recognition of land rights for racially oppressed indigenous people (1979).

The second function is administration of a *programme project list* circulated to churches and their agencies, seeking support for projects initiated by churches and other groups to combat racism. About $350,000 was raised and distributed in this manner in 1980 to work on race and minority issues in Asia, Indian movements in Latin America, land rights and racially oppressed groups, and ethnic minorities in Europe. In this area PCR and the Office of Education jointly sponsored a consultation, in part related to the International Year of the Child, which produced *The Slant of the Pen: Racism in Children's Books*.

The third function is the *Special Fund*, the separately administered (but thematically inter-related) programme of grants to organizations of the racially oppressed or groups that support them. This is where public attention has centred, because the grants, not in fact large amounts of money, are made publicly as symbols of solidarity. Not only, however, does this mean that PCR is thought of often only as the Special Fund but, as some WCC staff in other units sigh, so is the WCC.

The Special Fund has distributed about $4.8 million since its first grants in 1970. It is made up of specially designated gifts. In 1980 alone, gifts were received from Australia, Belgium, Canada, FRG, GDR, the Netherlands, New Zealand, Sweden, Switzerland, the UK, and the US. They came from member churches, local congregations, councils of churches, mission agencies, ecumenical groups and many individuals, as well as the governments of Sweden, Norway and the Netherlands. Since 1978 donors have been expected to provide an extra 10 per cent for the administration of the Fund, which means that neither the grants nor the administrative costs involve the regular WCC budget.

Among the criteria for the grants, adopted by the 1969 Central Committee and reconfirmed with minor verbal changes in 1976: the organizations must not be in conflict with the general purposes of the WCC and the grants are to be used for humanitarian activities; the grants are to be used to support organizations that combat racism and not those that undertake relief work, eligible for support elsewhere; the grants are made without control of the manner in which they are spent "as an expression of commitment by the PCR to the cause of economic, social and political justice, which these organizations support"; because of the overt nature of the racism there, Southern Africa is a priority.

Furore over grants

These grants had created simmering controversy — should the WCC take sides, was this supporting violence, who made the grant decisions anyway — but no one anticipated the firestorm that raged in August 1978, with the public announcement that a grant of $85,000 for humanitarian aid had been made to the Patriotic Front in Zimbabwe, at that time composed of the Zimbabwe African National Union (ZANU, headed by Robert Mugabe) and the Zimbabwean

African Peoples Union (ZAPU, headed by Joshua Nkomo) opposed to the solution being worked out by Bishop Abel Muzorewa (ANC, African National Congress) with the white minority.

The ANC, hailed in the West as a black-led solution to the civil conflict which had raged in Zimbabwe as the small white population tried to hold on to power, was in fact "dominated or ignored by the Ian Smith-led white members of government and the civil service", according to a professor of international relations at Hunter College, New York, who wrote at that time that it was only "preserving white privilege under a facade of black majority rule". That certainly was the judgment of those in the WCC who had decided a year earlier to end the grants to Muzorewa and to support the Patriotic Front.

The response was ferocious. "Killing for Christ", one liberal magazine headlined in the USA. A then out-of-work politician writing a column which ran in a number of newspapers wrote: "If those who dominate the WCC were reasonable, they would not be sending money to terrorists who kill civilians and missionaries. For now it seems to me that the best opportunity for reforming this radically minded organization which has so distorted the teachings of Christ is for individual church-goers to make sure that none of the financial support they give their own church goes to the WCC where it may end up as a bullet in a terrorist gun." The writer was Ronald Reagan, now US president.

He probably had read a publication by Ernest W. Lefever, *Amsterdam to Nairobi: the World Council of Churches and the Third World*. Lefever used the grant as a focus for an all-out attack on the WCC.

Lefever was nominated by Reagan to head the human rights desk at the US State Department in early 1981 but was rejected by the US Senate Foreign Relations Committee, the first time that action had occurred in this century. He withdrew as a candidate before almost certain rejection by the full US Senate. His book, translated into German, was sent to ministers in churches across Germany and Switzerland in 1981 by the South African embassy in Berne.

Much of the attack on the Council has been orchestrated by South Africa. This, however, does not explain everything. In late 1978 *Time* magazine carried a story on the grant with a picture of Philip Potter. The caption under Potter's picture read: "We can't help it if missionaries get killed." Only by reading the story could one discover that the quote came from an unrelated and unidentified "guerilla commander".

It was a painful time for Council staff and those in the churches defending the grants. For those in the situation, of course, things were much worse. Mrs Fred Shaw, wife of the Rev. Fred Shaw who heads the very anti-communist Christian League of South Africa, told one newspaper that the South African Council of Churches (SACC) had received millions of dollars from overseas and used the money to "distribute kits with directions on how to make bombs". When asked for evidence, she said the League did not yet have the documents. In early 1982 the SACC was under unremitting pressure from the government with legal investigations of its books and threats to cut off outside funds.

But the debate was on. One of the problems, British writer Barbara Rogers has suggested, was "the failure to involve the whole membership of the churches" before the fact. Few church members had the background information or experience necessary to interpret the often vicious attacks. "It would appear imperative that greater attention be given to the dissemination of information to the *membership,* not just the leaders, of the European and North American churches."

The debate within the churches was not easy. But several made formal motions of support. In the 1979 Assembly of the British Council of Churches a strong majority voted for a policy of "progressive disengagement" to replace the former concept of "constructive engagement" (investing in and trading with South Africa while trying to change conditions). Two congregations in FRG voted to contribute "church tax" money to the PCR in spite of opposition from their hierarchies.

The 1979 United Presbyterian Church (USA) general assembly, which admitted the grants had caused "confusion and concern in many congregations", after extensive briefing on the situation in Southern Africa and on PCR, offered "its deeply felt solidarity with the intentions and actions" of PCR.

When the Central Committee met in 1979, six months later, it called for a process of consultation, "in the light of the experience gained, the questions raised and the criticisms made during the ten years of PCR". Regional meetings in all parts of the world were to conclude with a world consultation.

From all reports, the national and regional meetings were significant events on their own, as the Australia experience would suggest. About 15 of these fed into the world consultation in the Netherlands, June 1980. Representatives came from member churches, race relations desks of various church bodies, and from oppressed groups.

These last voices "were a prominent and important feature" of the consultation, according to the final statement, because through them "we were reminded of the plight of millions of oppressed castes, ethnic and racial groups".

At its end the consultation on "Churches Responding to Racism in the 1980s" recommended — and the 1980 Central Committee later affirmed — "the continuation and strengthening of the PCR". Through it the churches have been helped to face the issue of racism and it should remain "an integral but distinct part" of the WCC's work. Without any change in the criteria, the Special Fund should "continue as an active expression of solidarity with the struggles against racism".

The Central Committee further urged its member churches and all Christians, using an appropriate mechanism, to "declare that apartheid is a sin which as a fundamental matter of faith is to be rejected as a perversion of the Christian gospel".

The report of the consultation is available from PCR and a personal critique of the process is recorded in Barbara Rogers's book *Race: No Peace Without Justice* (1980).

The consultative process, and the broader debate within the churches, have affirmed PCR. In both places stress was placed on better communication with more people within the churches, including providing the opportunity for churches and congregations to hear the stories of the oppressed themselves.

Fighting apartheid

One other area of action should be mentioned in this survey. Research has been continuous in PCR's life on the question of financial support for the South African government. The corporations and banks which invest there argue that at the least their investments are neutral, based on business criteria with no political implications, and at best investment creates prosperity which helps everyone. Bishop Desmond Tutu of the South African Council of Churches told the British Council of Churches in March 1981 that "foreign investors must know they are investing to buttress one of the most vicious systems since Nazism".

In September 1981, the WCC announced an end to its relations with three banks whose South African business was judged to be "supporting the system of racism embodied in apartheid".

This came after considerable discussion and correspondence, following policy first stated at the Uppsala Assembly in 1968 where the churches had directed the Council to end investments in "institutions that perpetuate racism". In 1974 the WCC closed an account with Midland Bank (UK) and the WCC US Conference closed an account with Citibank in New York earlier in 1981. Wesley Kenworthy, Assistant General Secretary for Finance and Administration for the WCC, said it was not a criticism of the excellent services offered by the three banks, Union Bank of Switzerland, the Swiss Bank Corporation and Dresdner Bank (FRG). Kenworthy, once an international banker himself, said it was necessary because the WCC must put "its own house in order". The objective is to foster "non-violent change towards a genuine multi-racial society" in South Africa.

The PCR, which plans a 1982 consultation with churches in Southern Africa to relate the programme's concerns more closely to the churches' priorities, received a sign of hope in late 1981. Obedience 81, a week-long gathering of 800 Methodists in Southern Africa, "called on every Methodist to reject apartheid".

Described as the largest and most representative gathering of Methodists in their 165-year history in this part of the world, the first few days, according to press reports, were marked by deep divisions between blacks and whites on the relationship of the church to political activities.

In the end, however, delegates unanimously accepted a list of concerns from the conference which included the unequivocal rejection of apartheid. "God seeks a free South Africa," part of a final statement says, "delivered from the violence of oppression, revolution and war.... What we have heard convinces us that every Methodist must witness against this disease which infects all our people and leaves none unscathed in our church and country....

"We have experienced", it continues, "how hard it is to abandon long-held prejudice and long-felt bitterness. But we have seen God work this miracle in us. It happened because we continued to search for each other even at our time of deepest division and despair."

CHAPTER 4

EDUCATION AND RENEWAL
IN SEARCH OF TRUE COMMUNITY

Ecumenism and the charismatic renewal

> I am cycling through B on a bicycle. Just near the school, I see a big house being built, higher than all the others. I dismount and think to myself: "This is it!" The sun is shining on its steep gables and the tower next to it. The workmen are hard at work. It won't be long until the roof is put on. There is something wrong with the gear transmission on my bicycle. It's not a big job to replace the broken screw.

She took no part in the discussions. She fasted. She prayed. And she offered a number of visions. It was not a typical moment in an ecumenical bark afloat in, among other things, a sea of words.

Another participant interpreted her vision:

> Perhaps the worldwide charismatic movement is the big, ecumenical house that is being built and we can say: "This is it." Beneath its roof Christians, who in the past have avoided one another — whether out of ignorance or fear — can perhaps learn to work together in mutual respect and fellowship. At any rate, that's what reports from all over the world seem to suggest.
>
> The trouble is that in me and many other observers there is obviously something wrong with the transmission. We are lagging behind with our "transmitting" and "understanding". There's a screw which needs replacing.

The visions were part of a 1980 consultation on the significance of charismatic renewal for the churches. About fifty people from member and non-member churches (including Roman Catholics) met "to clarify understanding of the charismatic renewal and its meaning for the churches, and to study the responses of the churches to the charismatic renewal".

The WCC's Sub-unit on Renewal and Congregational Life (RCL) working group had heard in 1978 Dr Arnold Bittlinger (FRG), a part-time consultant on the charismatic explosion, say that "a spiritual renewal unprecedented in the history of the Christian church has been spreading through the churches of the world since the beginning of the 1960s".

In contrast to other such movements, the "charismatic renewal" has reached all parts of the world, is within all confessions and among all social classes.

Bittlinger, who became involved twenty years ago when he was director of evangelism and stewardship for the United Church in the Federal Republic of Germany, dated the first "charismatic upsurge" from 1901 in Kansas City, USA. After tensions with the mother churches, this movement developed into the Pentecostals, embracing up to 40 million adherents and still growing.

A second charismatic "surge" began among Episcopalians, Lutherans and other Reformed churches in the US around 1960, found the Roman Catholic Church in 1967, and then spread throughout the world. It has been described as "neo-Pentecostalist", adopting much of the theology of the Pentecostalists but tending to remain within their churches. There is also a third group, "the charismatic congregational renewalists", also arising out of the 1960s, who "interpret their spiritual awakening in the light of and within the context of their own theological traditions. Nor do they establish prayer groups independently of their congregations (as 'neo-Pentecostalists' do); rather they seek to renew their own churches charismatically."

The RCL working group decided to hold the 1980 consultation and in preparation Philip Potter sent a letter to member churches asking them to share their experiences with the charismatic movement and help to formulate the questions the consultation would address. He received more than seventy official replies and said later: "I do not remember in the history of the Council any letter from the General Secretary so generously and copiously responded to — and that's saying something."

A number of people commented on the significance of the movement for the WCC itself. Here are three:

> Do not the workers and writers of ecumenical agreements need to look at the possibility that people in the charismatic renewal may have found a dimension of unity that they have not found?
>
> (The WCC cannot be a grassroots movement as long as it is based mainly on discussion.) The charismatic movement, in the few years of its existence, has begun to bring together, in significant numbers, the Catholic stream, the mainline Protestant stream, the evangelical Protestant stream, and the Pentecostal stream. This is exactly what Bishop Lesslie Newbigin had visualized in 1953 as a basic requirement for a renewed, missionary church.

You can create magnificent structures and models of what you see as the ultimate ecumenical church but it surely will fail if people are not made aware that the Holy Spirit himself is the real power who makes this happen.

At the beginning of the consultation Philip Potter acknowledged many charismatics might have problems with the WCC's holding such a meeting because of its image: too bureaucratic, too political, a forum for erudite scholars discussing obscure doctrines, a handmaiden of boards and agencies. But he affirmed the ecumenical movement itself as a renewal movement. He admitted that the ecumenical movement was dominated for a long time by the Augustinian emphasis on Christ. "There had been a deep lack of the work of the Holy Spirit in our life, and what that means for the unity of the church and the unity of the human community."

But he told the group about how the Orthodox, who had arrived in large numbers into the WCC only in 1961, insisted on changing the "basis" for membership to include the Trinity. Which was done, adding: "To the glory of the one God, Father, Son and Holy Spirit." From the Orthodox and from the charismatics have come a new understanding of the work of the Holy Spirit.

In the final report the participants recognized the need to watch for divisive tendencies in the charismatic renewal movement, but testified to the sense of community that developed during their time together, "melting reserve, destroying superiority, banishing fear, each esteeming the other better than oneself... Together we proclaim the unity of the church to be the Holy Spirit's gift and calling."

Gathering models of renewal

This is one of several ways in which Renewal and Congregational Life, formed after the Nairobi Assembly (incorporating the former Department of Laity), has attempted to work with the churches to formulate an understanding of "renewal" and "the congregation". The charismatic consultation and a 1978 seminar on worship were followed in 1981 by a meeting to discuss renewal in local congregations with a number of church members from the northern Pacific in a meeting held in Korea, and one in Zaire hosted by the Kimbanguist church. African spirituality was explored with African independent churches (many of them charismatic) through Bible study, worship, stories, music and pilgrimmage, rather than formal papers, discussions and the usual meeting-style speeches. All are part of the process of gathering models of renewal for sharing with the churches.

Canon David Tatchell (Canada), RCL Director since 1980, remembers that in Nairobi it was a kind of catch-phrase that the WCC doesn't get down to the local church, on the one hand; on the other, it doesn't hear what the churches are saying. "These two concerns were put together in this sub-unit."

Working with lay centres

Another way RCL works to fulfil its mission is through continuing contacts with lay centres and academies. They are different from the retreat centres formed around the order of common prayer, such as the Taizé community in France. They take many forms — they are, after all, in every part of the world — but generally are concerned about the life of the world, bringing together workers and politicians, specialists and generalists, and generally equipping laity for a ministry in the world.

For almost a decade more than two hundred groups have been in touch with one another through the World Collaboration Committee for Christian Lay Centres, Academies and Movements for Social Concern. The committee itself has 15 members, plans training programmes for staff, and meets almost annually. This has always been encouraged and supported by the WCC — the Rev. Carlos Sintado (Argentina) who, until 1980, directed such a centre in his home country, became the RCL staff person related to this specific concern.

Ecumenical education

RCL is one of five sub-units in what the WCC calls Unit III, Education and Renewal. By no means has this been the glamour unit of the Council. Ms Marie Assaad, who became Moderator of Unit III in 1980, was puzzled upon her arrival to find that the importance of the work of this unit with *people* was not really understood. "When you look at other units, you think first of issues, then programmes, then people. It is our task to think first of people and their concerns."

The main task of this unit has been described as "enabling people to participate in the new community, the community where in Christ there is neither Jew nor Greek, there is neither slave nor free, there is neither male nor female" (Gal. 3:28).

Ms Assaad is from the Coptic Church in Egypt and remembers the early euphoria about the ecumenical movement, the curiosity and excitement in getting to know one another. This gave way to another stage, and another important discovery: "When the churches got together, they realized that actual unity is something to look forward to but is not as easy as first hoped."

And something else happened. "When the churches got together, prayed and worked together, the prophetic role became very clear. They could not evade the struggles for social justice."

But she feels from her own church's experience there was a problem. While this was taking place, "the ecumenical experience moved very far ahead of our member churches. Too few networks around the world know what we are talking about, read our literature, communicate with us. Because a language and jargon have developed that became limited to those with the experience of ecumenical solidarity."

Nairobi guidelines called for a truly ecumenical fellowship. For this to happen, all WCC programmes should be conceived and carried out in a manner enabling member churches "to grow towards a truly ecumenical, conciliar fellowship", and churches must be helped to participate "in the process of ecumenical education".

Seeking a definition of such ecumenical education, Ms Assaad has posed a set of questions. What does ecumenical learning really mean? How can the local communities participate in the ecumenical movement? If people learn more from involvement than reading pieces of paper, how can such experiences be created? How can people participate and share the experiences of others, a global vision, while remaining not only rooted but committed to a specific culture?

Many of the questions asked here are the specific stuff of the work of the Sub-unit on *Education*, another element of the WCC with a storied ecumenical history. The Sunday school movement celebrated its 200th birthday in 1980. Various Sunday school conventions formed the World Sunday School Association in Rome in 1907. It met in various countries every four years and, as the World Council on Christian Education, moved its office to Geneva in the 1960s where it worked closely with the youth and education offices of the WCC. At its 1971 assembly the WCCE voted formally to merge with the WCC.

Dr Ulrich Becker (FRG), who taught religious education in his own country before becoming director of the Education sub-unit, said he has been "moved" by the hope people in some parts of the world place on the educational role. The educational boom of the 1960s and early 1970s in North America and Europe has faded as new uncertainties and doubts have arisen. But there is "still much trust in education in developing countries. After all, a person who can read and write has a different future from one who does not."

According to Becker, the education office is often interpreted as a communications arm of the programmes of the Council. How does the church appropriate the theological agreements worked out in

Faith and Order on baptism, eucharist and ministry? What are the best ways for the churches to begin to grasp the mission that is now in each and every place, as CWME believes? What kind of education reaches specific groups: congregations, groups, adults, youth? Becker believes the problem is well reflected in traditional seminary education, where Old and New Testaments are studied separately, as are church history, dogmatics, systematic theology, ethics. At the end, often, practical theology is tacked on. "I believe in a dialectical arrangement, an involvement in educational action that raises new theological questions, questions that might not have arisen without the practical involvement. The recent discussions of children and communion, for example, did not come out of theology but from the reflections on daily work with children."

The sub-unit divides its work into several priorities, one of which is *adult basic education*. For ten years until 1980 this was the place where the remarkable educationalist Paulo Freire (Brazil) shared his understanding of the use of literacy training with adults as a form of personal empowerment. He calls it *conscientization*. It is the process by which people in situations of oppression are enabled to become aware of the causes of their condition. It helps them, in turn, to break out of the oppressive structures in which they live. Paulo Freire's theories have greatly influenced programmes of education, especially of non-formal adult education, in the WCC and around the world.

A second priority is *ecumenical learning*. Here specific wrestling goes on with some of Marie Assaad's questions. One goal, not an unambitious one, would be to encourage a creative combining of the traditional teacher-oriented and the new action-oriented education. Another is to collect "common catechetical programmes", curricula developed jointly by different confessional families.

Yet another priority: *church-related educational institutions*. Nairobi asked the WCC to assist churches in evaluating the role of their educational institutions, primary, secondary, vocational, university. Should they continue to be a priority? If so, are the consistent charges of elitism, of failing to serve the poor, correct? (In Washington DC three of the most expensive and elitist secondary schools are church-run.)

The staff have participated in (and at times stimulated) a number of regional meetings on these issues. A dossier from those experiences, dealing with the theological basis and present priorities of church-related educational institutions, has received considerable circulation. The answers coming in vary widely with the country and the socio-political situation.

In India the Christian 2.5 per cent (still more than 15 million) supports 10,000 primary schools, 2,000 secondary schools, 174 colleges, 273 technical schools and 25 institutions for the disabled. Ms Doris Franklin, Associate Secretary for the Council of Christian Education in India, argues in the dossier that they remain an important service to all of India. When millions never enter school and only one out of every one hundred who enter school is able to reach the tenth grade, "the church should not only hold on to its institutions, but turn them into launching grounds for the fight against social discrimination and injustice".

Whatever the position taken in this published debate, most would agree with the Filipino who said that church-related schools should "sharply focus their mission and efforts towards the underprivileged of our society". He called that a vivid contrast to government policy.

A fourth priority is the *scholarship and leadership* programme. One of the oldest aid projects, this traditional form of help, as with all else, is undergoing change so as to meet the needs of the time. The scholarship programme is not intended for individuals to further their studies, but — and the 1980 Central Committee reaffirmed this — it should be an educational process for the churches, helping them to plan for the ministries considered important for themselves and their communities.

In the past, applications came to Geneva where a committee decided on the average of 180 scholarships awarded each year. Now, in part influenced by the discussion of ecumenical sharing of resources, churches in a particular country are encouraged to set up an ecumenical scholarships committee, so that together they may work out priorities and select suitable candidates. Problems remain with this change, not least that some churches have not yet entered the process, meaning that potential students from their country may have no chance for financial aid. The scholarships are open to women and men, ordained or lay, with a bias towards an ecumenical dimension (but not necessarily theological studies) and for those engaged in church service, community service, or seeking further theological training.

Biblical Studies continue under the very special leadership of Dr Hans-Ruedi Weber (Switzerland) who came to the Council in 1955. Dr Weber, who has achieved considerable success helping people to find new ways to approach the Bible, completed in 1981 a handbook for biblical exploration, *Experiments with Bible Study*. The author examines in the first part of the book how the biblical message has guided the life of Christians in different centuries and cultures. The second part contains examples of Bible studies which make use of the rich variety of approaches explored in different confessions and continents.

(The concern for the Bible is not isolated at one place within the Council. For example, CWME worked with the United Bible Societies to produce an issue of its *International Review of Mission* on "The Bible in Mission" in 1981 and F&O prepared *The Bible: its Authority and Interpretation in the Ecumenical Movement* in 1980. The study resources *Images of Life*, published in preparation for the forthcoming Assembly, are based on seven evocative biblical images which focus on the theme "Jesus Christ — the Life of the World".)

"If there's a communication failure in the family, then of course the faith can't be shared. Ninety-nine per cent of those in the church today are there because they were nurtured in Christian families. The faith can't be shared in the neighbourhood, the church and the community when it's not shared in the family to start with," said Leslie Clements of New Zealand who directed the World Council's *Family Life Education* programme for nine years until 1977.

The family education programme, now headed by Ma Mpolo Masamba (Zaire), has involved the Council in a variety of relationships with society's basic unit. In cooperation with churches and Christian councils, it has been helping to train people in basic marriage counselling skills and family life education. It has supported and encouraged "families healing families", through various models, like the family cluster model, marriage encounter and the Christian family movement. Workshops reflecting on such issues as adolescent pregnancies, sex identity and human relationships, responsible parenthood, preparation for marriage, abortion, population education and the quality of life, have helped to increase the awareness of churches.

Since 1976, an innovative experiment called the Family Power Social Change Project has been tried. About 52 family groups — including one-parent families and single people — were brought together in 35 different countries to discuss ways they can operate with more strength to make an impact on their societies. In a 1980 world meeting of these families in Oaxtepec, Mexico, they identified a number of issues affecting their families, such as tourism, prostitution, inflation, unemployment, and meagre family incomes, some of which they would like to tackle jointly. The creation and support of regional family movements were also proposed as a possible means of sharing experiences and participating in the encouragement of supportive relationships in favour of families.

Ongoing studies in member churches on church and child, the 1979 International Year of the Child and the bicentennial of the Sunday school movement in 1980 have proved important ways of reconsidering the church's ministry with children. This programme priority laid specific emphasis on helping churches rethink their theological understanding of childhood and assess the place of children in the church, in its sacramental, worshipping and congregational life.

Theological education

Theological education, understandably, is one of the major priorities of the Council. From 1958 to 1977, the Theological Education Fund (TEF), lodged in CWME, played a crucial role in the strengthening of theological education in the third world. At the 1976 Central Committee, the decision was taken to transform TEF into an independent sub-unit called the Programme on Theological Education (PTE).

PTE's scope is broader. The task of the Fund, for the most part, was to provide assistance for theological education projects in third world countries. In the words of Aharon Sapsezian (Brazil) who heads the new sub-unit, PTE "will be involved in the efforts to renew theological education and ministerial training in all six continents — therefore also in the northern hemisphere".

The definitive mandate for the PTE was adopted during the 1977 Central Committee meeting. It emphasized that the PTE's primary concern was to enhance an ecumenical vision in theological education. Practical training for the ministry of the churches, lay or ordained, women and men, was to be the focus of the new sub-unit's operations. Funding should continue, and it should be concentrated on five areas of need, described as:
— creative undertakings where original, seminal and contextual theological reflection and writing are taking place;
— associations and regional bodies on theological education;
— the continuing search for new patterns of theological learning and ministerial formation suitable to the cultural, social and economic context;
— the training of national teaching personnel;
— intra- and inter-regional exchange of students and teachers.

Immediately following 1977, the PTE launched a series of international consultations which are expressive of its new nature and mandate. Significantly the first of these was one on Orthodox Theological Education (Basel, July 1978), which brought together for the first time representatives of Orthodox theological schools in Europe, the Middle East, India and North America. One of the key recommendations of this consultation was the creation of an Orthodox Association for Theological Education, and efforts have since been made to implement it.

The following year, a worldwide consultation on Ministerial Formation was held in Tagaytay City, near Manila, Philippines (July 1979). Its purpose was not to establish certain patterns or even to define set concepts of ministerial formation; it was to challenge the churches and their institutions not to be satisfied with the assumptions and practices of the past but to look afresh at the basic issues and necessary components within their own particular contexts as they face the future.

In October 1980 a key consultation was held in the German Democratic Republic on European theological education. One of the surprising realizations in this consultation was that Europe, despite its many ecumenical structures and networks, was very poorly equipped to share experiences, problems and expectations in the field of theological education and programmes for the preparation of the ministry of the churches. During the consultation, participants looked at Europe as one context among many in the world, a context which would welcome insights and lessons from theological education practices in other parts of the world. This attitude would enable people to look critically at some typically European problems like the scientific approach in theological education, the accountability of theological education to the church, and the ecumenical components of theological education.

The last of the series of international consultations took place in July 1981 in Toronto, Canada. This Canadian/US consultation had for its theme "Global Solidarity in Theological Education". It challenged those responsible for theological education in that part of the world to relate more directly with contemporary issues of international justice and the quest for peace, and to reinterpret theological education in the light of such issues.

The PTE also continued to exercise its service in the field of financial assistance, mainly in third world areas, but also in underprivileged pockets within the economically rich nations. PTE-assisted projects were normally of a relatively small size — between roughly $1,000 and $15,000 each. In the five years of its operation, assistance has been provided for 365 projects, totalling nearly $1.7 million. A great deal of encouragement has been given to the consolidation of the work of the thirty or so associations of theological schools around the world; these associations have a great potential for ecumenical coordination and joint undertakings. Alternative methods and patterns of theological education, like theological education by extension, were greatly expanded during the period. This development is described in the two publications, *The Extension Movement in Theological Education and Ministry by the People.*

"To enable youth together"

Nairobi put a heavy emphasis on setting up WCC youth work, "so as to enable youth together to discover for themselves the freedom and unity in Christ, to voice their concerns and insights effectively, and to participate at all levels of the ecumenical movement, particularly in the WCC. The focus should seek to bring the challenges and concerns of youth into the central life of the WCC in all aspects of its work." Three major concerns of youth were identified: youth and theology, youth and education, and youth and social justice. The suggested functions and programme emphases also highlighted the need for young people to share with each other and develop their own directions rather than being told what to do: develop means of contact with youth; develop a network of communication among youth; create opportunities for youth to meet across national, regional and confessional boundaries to share their common insights; promote programmes among rural youth. Also noted was the need for constant advocacy of the concern of youth within the WCC "so as to achieve adequate representation in all committees, commissions, programmes and staff of the WCC".

The background to these was an illustrious history followed by a spectacular collapse of the WCC Youth Department. The situation had deteriorated so badly that even the very existence of WCC youth work was in doubt at Nairobi.

The near fatal accident had taken place following the powerful presence on the fringe of the 1968 Assembly at Uppsala, when it was felt that instead of a strong independent youth department, it would be better to "integrate" youth into the whole life and work of the WCC. The first phase of integration — reduction of the Youth Department — was successfully carried out. The second phase never happened. And in the years up to Nairobi, as in a number of major denominations, youth work virtually disappeared.

Nairobi was therefore a time of hope for youth, following the period of near despair, and there was a strong positive response to the reaffirmation of the WCC youth work.

Sub-unit Director Peter Moss (UK: Northern Ireland) quotes two statements from major ecumenical leaders to illustrate the sense of urgency for effective youth work and the resistance to it. Said a Latin

95

American church leader at the 1976 WCC Central Committee: "We have lost a whole generation of young people." Said an African church leader in 1982: "As soon as you nominate a youth for something, the church leader thinks it is aimed against him." By the time the first statement was made, says Moss, the effects of the second were already becoming evident. At that meeting the Central Committee set up the working groups and commissions to review the sub-unit programmes and policies until the next assembly — with a very low representation of youth. This led to a youth proposal which was accepted, that "all future commissions, committees and working groups appointed by the Central Committee reflect at least the percentage of women, laity and youth at the Fifth Assembly". This meant that about 10% should be youth. (Youth in WCC terms means 16-30 years old, a compromise between very different concepts in different parts of the world. The range goes from North Americans agonizing over their lost youth at the age of 19 to Orthodox people signing up for youth conferences at 75 years. The current record is a highly active member of a Samoan youth group who is a cool 82!)

During 1977 and 1978 the sub-unit tested out different ways of working. A key element was visitation to different regions and the beginning of a new youth network, including a new newsletter called *Youth*.

Another experiment was the sending of a group of young people as participants to the Faith and Order Commission meeting in Bangalore, India, in 1978. It was another valuable sharing experience, but very little impression was made on the theological establishment, reports the Director, and the encounter revealed the gulf between the youth urge for unity and the intellectual route being taken at the official level to achieve, postpone or avoid it. The group dealing with issues of youth at the F&O meeting said:

> Youth should not be regarded as a special category — they are fully a part of the people of God; nor are they the "church of tomorrow" but members of today's church. They are not confined to so-called youth issues, but as part of the universal community of faith confront all the problems facing humanity today.

Up to 1977, five regional ecumenical youth movements (Africa, Asia, the Caribbean, Europe and Latin America) related to the WCC. By 1979 they had been joined by the Middle East, North America and the Pacific. The first joint meeting between working group members and the regional secretaries took place in Beirut in 1979. There it was agreed to build an "ecumenical youth fellowship" through active cooperation between the WCC and the regional youth movements, especially the development of a programme of regional, inter-regional and international events. At the meeting they discussed at length the issues and priorities of young people in all eight regions. Two main areas were identified — faith (what does it mean to believe in Jesus Christ today?) and justice (how do we as young people struggle together for justice in today's world?). It was agreed to take "Faith and Justice" as the overall theme for future programmes. Under the agreement each region naturally continued its own programme, but a two-year series of events was put together on a cooperative basis, with the provision for some representatives from other regions to attend.

Encouragement for the scheme came from the 1978 success of the "Christian Youth in a Troubled Society" meeting which had been jointly organized by the WCC and the Middle East Council of Churches youth offices and had given a major boost to the new MECC youth programme.

The first regional meeting (Latin America, July 1979) illustrated the shared possibilities and the shared pain involved in such cooperation. All the other regions except Asia sent representatives and the sharing of experiences and insights was powerful. There was a real sense of fellowship covering both personal and institutional relations. Young people's involvement in struggles for justice was highlighted, ironically, by the absence of the Nicaraguan delegation.

Nicaragua had just achieved liberation and there was deep rejoicing at the victory and the role youth had played. A real sense of optimism filled the air.

A different reality was to follow, however, as, within a few months of returning home, the whole delegation from El Salvador disappeared. They had been involved in working with the community, setting up medical posts and in various ways helping the people. This was but one of many examples of the cost of discipleship. From the permanent disappearance of a young woman activist in the Philippines, the murder and torture of many young people in South Korea, discrimination and suffering in Southern Africa, a new generation has become aware of the cost of commitment.

The next meeting, bringing together young Christians from seven countries, in Southern Africa, re-emphasized the challenges and the calling. Half-way through the meeting, the radio news announced that Robert Mugabe had won the elections in Zimbabwe and the delegates from that country virtually exploded in joy at the knowledge that now they were free. Almost a full day of celebration,

97

dancing, singing and worship followed, with all the participants joining in fervently. And at the same time, the tales of exclusion and discrimination, and concern for the young freedom fighters who must now readjust their lives, gave a sense of reality to the theme of "The Role of Youth in Liberation and Nation-building".

The following meetings, while also furthering inter-regional sharing (a process which continues to develop), raised their own issues. Unity was one of them. Young people from Africa, Europe and the Middle East, after studying oppression in the political, social and economic fields, as well as the relations between rich and less rich churches, issued a strong warning against too-easy assumptions of unity. Unity, they said, could not be realized without the elimination of the injustices which divided rich from poor, powerful from powerless in the churches as well as between nations.

While they were meeting in Cyprus, the largest-ever international gathering of Orthodox youth was taking place in Finland, organized by SYNDESMOS, the World Fellowship of Orthodox Youth Organizations. The participants in the festival passed two significant resolutions, one calling on the heads of Orthodox churches to do whatever is possible to solve the problem of the diaspora, the other asking heads of Orthodox and Oriental Orthodox churches to accelerate steps towards full unity of these two families of Orthodoxy.

The various unity strands were pulled together early in 1981 in a mountain-top monastery in Syria when a joint Orthodox-Protestant youth meeting was convened by SYNDESMOS and the WCC Youth sub-unit. With the theme "To be a Servant", it brought together some of the experiences from the "Faith and Justice" and the SYNDESMOS "Witness and Service" meetings. It challenged people to consider the nature of Christian witness, especially how far it is expressed in social and political action. And it challenged the Orthodox in particular to greater openness towards those of other traditions. A full and constructive encounter, it deepened and broadened this particular ecumenical dialogue, which holds great possibilities for the future.

Before moving into the phase of all-out Assembly preparations, a "Faith and Justice" course concluded the two-year programme initiated in Beirut. Held in Turin, Italy, it brought together delegations from each region and SYNDESMOS, each delegation being given an equal number of places. It was an exciting encounter. Participants recognized the church as a key base in the struggle for justice and challenged the church to involve itself in people's struggles and to take action for renewal and unity. "Faith and Justice" seemed to represent the living experience of the participants and those in their movements.

In planning the youth event which will immediately precede the Assembly, the hope is to harness the new strength and enable the youth voice to be heard "in the midst of intellectuals and holy people wearing fascinating ecclesiastical costumes and ornamentations" as one of the Pacific youth leaders said in Turin. Up to 300 young Assembly participants will be there. Most of them will be delegates or stewards. Only the delegates will have full speaking and voting rights. Yet the stewards represent the youth movement at least as fully as the delegates. They are the serving ones who keep the Assembly running by performing all manner of tasks. They also always develop their own spirit and programme.

Enabling young people together to make their voice heard remains at the heart of the sub-unit's commitment. The role of delegates and stewards together will testify to that in Vancouver.

Dialogue in community

Syncretism, said the critics at the Nairobi Assembly. Dialogue with neighbours of other faiths risks selling out the uniqueness of the Christian faith, compromises its exclusive claims, risks the danger of syncretism, blending elements of several religions into one.

Not so, said its defenders. The critics came primarily from Europe and North America. Those who affirmed dialogue were largely Asians and Africans where the churches have for generations existed with other faiths as part of a larger community.

The Rev. Lynn de Silva, for two decades director of a study centre with long experience in dialogue with the Buddhist majority in his country of Sri Lanka, told the Assembly that the fears and anxieties he had heard appeared to come mainly from people who had never encountered or lived among people of other faiths. He affirmed dialogue in the following ways (his words are paraphrased and summarized):

Dialogue enriches and strengthens one's faith rather than diminishing it.

Dialogue is a safeguard against syncretism, not a temptation, because in dialogue we get to know one another's faith in depth which tests and sharpens one's own faith.

Dialogue is a creative interaction liberating a person from a closed or cloistered system, perhaps simply inherited from an accident of birth, offering spiritual freedom which promises a richer spiritual life.

Dialogue is urgent and essential for us in Asia in order to repudiate the arrogance, aggression and negativism of our evangelistic crusades which have obscured the gospel and caricatured Christianity as an aggressive and militant religion.

Dialogue is essential to dispel the negative attitude we have of people of other faiths which makes proclamation ineffective and irrelevant. A negative attitude invites a negative response.

From the earliest days of the church, Christians have been living with people of other faiths. Various modes of cooperation, tension, suspicion, misunderstanding and even persecution mark that relationship. Within the ecumenical movement, the attitude to take towards "non-Christians" was discussed as early as Edinburgh.

Since 1971 that discussion has been carried out within the WCC by a special sub-unit on Dialogue with People of Living Faiths and Ideologies (DFI).

Without question those involved with DFI were surprised and even shaken by the hostility expressed by some towards dialogue in the Nairobi Assembly. But Dr Stanley Samartha (India), who directed the programme for its first ten years, believes that in retrospect the controversy proved to be more of an opportunity than a setback. "Instead of leading to a premature demise of dialogue, it helped to strengthen it as an ecumenical concern by drawing pointed attention to serious issues that are important to the life of churches, not just in Asia, but in other parts of the world as well."

In fact, the understanding of dialogue taking place in community has been affirmed in the period since Nairobi. That crisis has passed, and dialogue will continue to be integral to the ecumenical approach.

In "Guidelines on Dialogue" the relation to community is described:

> Dialogue, therefore, is a fundamental part of Christian service within community. In dialogue Christians actively respond to the command to love God and your neighbour as yourself. As an expression of love engagement in dialogue testifies to the love experienced in Christ. It is a joyful affirmation of life against chaos, and a participation with all who are allies of life in seeking the provisional goals of a better human community. Thus "dialogue in community" is not a secret weapon in the armoury of an aggressive Christian militancy. Rather it is a means of living our faith in Christ in service of community with one's neighbours.

That, incidentally, is the reason the discussion of dialogue is placed here under education, renewal and true human community. In the WCC structure DFI is in the unit on Faith and Witness.

Samartha doesn't use the word "non-Christian". "Dialogue is with neighbours of other faiths," he believes.

His distinction is more than academic. Non-Christian is a negative term, a bit triumphalist — "a hidden assumption that we are true and they are false" — and unscientific, because it is plainly inaccurate to lump together religions as different as Buddhism and Islam.

The shift reflects a new stage of understanding, one where listening to and being involved with people who are "other" is important, a shift that is reflected in other WCC programmes where the work is no longer for the poor, but with; no longer for those of colour, but with; no longer about women, but with.

What occurred before Nairobi has been described by some participants as more of an "internal dialogue" among the churches on the issue of dialogue. What has taken place since Nairobi is the affirmation of dialogue with neighbours of other faiths and ideologies.

Lessons learned from the involvement of an even larger number of church members in those dialogues have made an impact on the total work of the Council and member churches. It is also important that the Vatican Secretariat for Non-Christians, which grew out of Vatican II and its own concern for dialogue, has worked closely with DFI since its formal creation in 1971.

This period has put to rest the question raised directly by some at Nairobi about whether the programme should even exist. The key moment came at a meeting held in Chiangmai, Thailand, in 1977 called "Dialogue in Community". (The full report is in a book called *Faith in the Midst of Faiths*.) It involved 85 participants from 36 countries from the various WCC streams, with Roman Catholic and evangelical guests.

From Chiangmai — where Buddhists shared with the group, took them on visits to their "wats", and "provided opportunities for participants to sense, feel, and sometimes to understand what 'community' meant to them as Buddhists" — came a statement on dialogue. After revisions based upon responses from the churches, this became, in 1979 action by the Central Committee, "Guidelines on Dialogue with People of Living Faiths and Ideologies". The Guidelines, published in several languages, have been widely distributed and reviewed.

The lessons learned and the experiences shared in the debate leading up to the agreement of the importance of dialogue and the adoption of the "Guidelines" have obviously made an impact on the self-understanding of the WCC. The "Guidelines", for example, mention the close relationship between the concern for dialogue and work for visible church unity.

Beyond following up on the implications of dialogue for the churches through discussions about the guidelines, DFI has continued to organize bilateral dialogues. For example, 1981 saw a bilateral dialogue between Hindus and Christians, a meeting convened in India in cooperation with the Indian NCC, the Orthodox Church in India, the Church of North India, and with full participation of the Catholic Bishops' Conference of India. It also brought together Hindus and Christians who live alongside each other in Sri Lanka, Malaysia, Indonesia (Bali), South Africa, Kenya, the Caribbean, Western Europe, and the US around the theme: "Religious Resources for a Just Society."

For some of the Hindus present, it was the first opportunity they had had to discuss Hindu life in other societies. For all, it was a special experience. A report from the meeting told of a communications gap beyond the usual one of different languages in WCC meetings. "Sometimes we could not understand each other... but we discovered that there is much we can do together. Gradually we came to the realization that dialogue has to do with relationships; it is a way of living."

In 1981 were also formulated guidelines for Jewish-Christian dialogue, the completion of a four-year process of circulating drafts and holding small meetings by the Consultation on the Church and the Jewish People (CCJP). This group worked closely with the International Jewish Committee on Interreligious Consultations.

This, too, is an ecumenical milestone, overcoming as it had to a number of historical tensions. At one point the guidelines recognize that:

> Christians cannot enter into dialogue with Jews without the awareness of anti-Semitism and its long persistent history, especially in countries where Jews constitute a minority among Christians. (Ed. note: Anti-Semitism was condemned in Amsterdam in 1948 as a "sin against God and man", an idea reiterated many times.) Christians must face honestly the tragic history of anti-Semitism, which includes the crusades, the Inquisition, pogroms and the Holocaust. It is only by facing this history that Christians can understand the deep-rooted suspicion that many Jews even today have of Christians and Christianity.

Dialogue between the two faiths is of special importance because of "the ways in which Christianity historically emerged out of Judaism". But that also presents problems because Christians often believe they "know" Judaism. Yet too often that knowledge is deformed "by lack of knowledge about the history of Jewish life and thought through the 1900 years since the parting of the ways of Judaism and Christianity" and because what is known is too often defined by *Christian* teachers and preachers.

Participants in dialogue must be allowed to testify "in their own terms" in order to understand, for example, "the bond between the Land of Israel and the Jewish people. This bond has, after many centuries of dispersion, found expression in the State of Israel. The need for the State of Israel to exist in security and peace is fundamental to Jewish consciousness and therefore is of paramount importance in any dialogue with Jews."

At the same time Christians come into dialogue with Jews aware of the need to hear Christians and Muslims who, as Palestinians, describe their tie to the land "in their own terms" also.

> These attachments to the Land only emphasize the need for sustained dialogue with Jews. In such dialogue, consideration should be given to finding ways to promote mutual respect and reconciliation among Jews, Christians and Muslims in the Middle East and elsewhere as a contribution to the common welfare of all members of God's human family.

Beneath those words lies the continuing tension between the WCC's consistent position that the rights of Palestinians must be addressed before a just settlement is possible and Jewish feelings that such statements have often reflected at best little sympathy with the precariousness of Israel and at worst implicit anti-Semitism.

Early 1982 brought a Christian-Muslim consultation, on "The Ethics and Practices of Humanitarian and Development Programmes". This was the first time that the WCC had cooperated with a world Islamic organization, the World Muslim Congress, in such a dialogue, although the congress and other organizations had taken part in planning meetings in 1976 and 1979 when mutually agreed principles for dialogue had been accepted. Dialogues had also been arranged with Muslim scientists in Beirut in 1977 and with Muslim young people, mostly students and teachers, in Geneva in 1980. In a decade of exceptional tension and open conflict between Christians and Muslims in many parts of the world, it has been more than ever necessary to have the nerve and vision to continue and develop Christian-Muslim relations. The hundred Christians who met in Mombasa in December 1979 made recommendations on "Christian Presence and Witness in Relation to Muslim Neighbours" which were commended to the churches for study and action by the subsequent Central Committee.

Buddhists have been involved in several multilateral dialogues but only one bilateral dialogue with Buddhists has been sponsored by DFI. It took place in 1978 on "Religious Dimensions in Humanity's Relations to Nature"; the findings are published in *Man in Nature: Guest or Engineer.*

An important development during this period is the increased interest in dialogue shown by Western churches. Most so far had limited their concern to modest support for study centres in Asia who were the standard-bearers for dialogue. The growing presence of Hindus, Buddhists and Muslims in their own societies and the resurgence of Islam have introduced particular intensity to this. For the first time many Western churches have created special instruments for dialogue. The Conference of European Churches, for example, has held several meetings with Muslims living in Europe.

African Christians, Pacific Christians and indigenous peoples of the Americas have at various times been brought to share what it is like to come from their own cultures into an encounter with Christianity.

Finally, a meeting on "Churches among Ideologies" was held in December 1981. Stanley Samartha listed, before his departure, the inadequate work done on the "I" in DFI as a shortcoming of recent years. In Nairobi delegates from Africa and Asia had complained that too little had been made of the varieties of ideology which in fact have a major impact on the unity of the church. They deplored the tendency to see ideology only in the primary institutionalized forms, "whether liberal capitalism or Marxist socialism". DFI, without funds to staff "ideology", stimulated about 15 study groups around the world to discuss this issue and feed into the December conference.

Dr John B. Taylor (UK), now director of DFI, said in late 1981:

> Our neighbours in the modern world clearly include people loyal to secular ideologies or nationalist ideologies which, if not always well defined, are there in presuppositions. This is one of the elements that creates divisions among churches and yet, creatively, it can help bring them together also. We used to think that the faith was inside, ideology outside. Now we know that ideology is often in both places just as, glory be, faith is.

As it turned out, church people from twenty-seven different nations came to the ideologies consultation in December 1981. They came for what they described as an "internal" dialogue about their highly diverse ideological situations. Addressing a difficult problem, which had been a sticking point in earlier attempts at approaching the question of ideologies, they used as a working definition the idea that "ideology is a system of thought or blue-print used to interpret society and the individual's place in society, the function of which is either to legitimate the existing structures of society or to change them".

Use of that definition helped the participants to understand more clearly that none of them — and none of the churches from which they came — lived without ideological assumptions, too often unexamined.

When the working group of the DFI received the still unedited report of the consultation, it urged other units and sub-units of the WCC, and also the member churches, to continue to explore the ramifications of ideologies and ideological reflection on their ongoing work. Further, the DFI urged that sufficient resources, in finance and personnel, be provided in order for it to develop adequately its mandate to engage in "external" dialogue with persons who identify themselves primarily in terms of ideologies.

Health in community

The churches in Sierra Leone had a problem. For years they had invested money and talent in their medical work. But the Christian minority in this nation of under five million in West Africa knew that what they were doing had to be re-examined. Like churches the world over, they were aware that rising costs in their hospitals limited their ministries. Their training programmes were not as effective in reaching those who needed care most.

Word had reached them that churches in other countries, such as Ghana and Malawi, had formed coordinating agencies which met to discuss among themselves, and with the government, plans for improving health care, especially in rural areas, central purchasing of supplies, including ever-more-costly pharmaceutical items. When in 1975 the Christian Medical Commission (CMC) of the WCC planned a meeting in Kenya of such coordinating agencies in Africa, the Sierra Leone churches asked to be included. From Sierra Leone came a Methodist, a Roman Catholic and a woman doctor working for the government.

Within six weeks of the meeting, those in the Sierra Leone churches wrote to the CMC asking if it could provide a person to do a survey to help them explore options for creating such a coordinating agency.

CMC sent Dr Stuart Kingma (USA), then new to the staff and now CMC Director (replacing Dame Nita Barrow, Barbados, so instrumental in developing the current CMC approach). Kingma spent a month in Sierra Leone visiting both government and church hospitals and clinics, and talking with medical and church personnel. He made his report to a national workshop. It decided to form a coordinating committee. All the main actors were involved — Methodists, Roman Catholics, Seventh Day Adventists — and government representatives sat in. The government is closely tied to the resulting coordinating committee, which quickly hired an executive secretary and a small staff, standardized grant procedures, and embarked on a cooperative pharmaceutical purchasing and distribution service.

An interesting test of the new relationship occurred when the government raised its standards for training of nurses and midwives. Neither the Methodist hospital, which had enrolled nurse and midwifery training, nor the Catholic hospital at the other end of the country with registered nurse and midwifery training, could meet the new standards. So the two combined their programmes to meet standards neither could meet alone. Jointly they have embarked on the training of a new type of health worker, the "community-health enrolled nurse" (a nurse midwife). The government is paying a substantial part of the bill and the results are exciting.

This collaboration has led to a number of other imaginative ventures, including workshops on the church's healing ministry, ways of providing community or primary health care, and structures for dealing with the pharmaceutical question.

Such stories can be repeated for countries like Botswana, India, Tanzania, Guatemala, Pakistan and Nigeria. When Papua New Guinea became a new nation in 1972, with enormous health needs, the government there could not find the kind of consultant it wanted until it approached the CMC. Dr Håkan Hellberg (Finland), then the Associate Director of CMC, was seconded to the Ministry of Health for nine months to survey both government and church medical experience. With government approval, he constructed a plan that integrated the two. It also included a church-government liaison officer for medical concerns who is an appointee of the Ministry of Health. That relationship continues.

This is just one aspect of the work of the Christian Medical Commission, a sub-unit of the WCC which has been in existence only since 1968. Its origins reach back almost a decade earlier when the churches and mission boards operating in all parts of the world began to face a crucial issue. The medical programmes of the Christian church, with its proclaimed bias on behalf of the poor, were primarily directed at hospitals increasingly available only to the rich. The escalating costs of maintaining large hospitals, with rising salaries, ever more expensive drugs and costly technology, were limiting who could use them. In the early days CMC research suggested that on average 80 per cent of the people in the developing countries had no access to medical care. This became an increasing challenge to local churches and to mission boards who had always "reached the unreached" and gone where others would not. (The World Health Organization later confirmed the CMC data and recent studies do not suggest much easing of the problem.)

CMC originated out of the need for the churches to begin to deal with these facts. It was seen as a way to talk together rather than to struggle in isolation, with a lot of hard practical and, at first, institutional problems.

But CMC was not conceived simply to address the institutional question of hospital costs. Its mandate is "to serve as an advisory and consultative agency to the churches around the world as they seek to carry out their healing ministry".

As the churches, and a large number of those involved in seeking better ways of providing health especially in areas where it is difficult, began to work together even before the creation of CMC, they sought a clearer understanding of the biblical and theological foundation for the churches' involvement in health care.

In the past too much emphasis had been placed on curing diseases through doctors, drugs and care in hospitals, largely in urban areas. The CMC approach calls for much more emphasis on preventive services and on the promotion and preservation of health. The local community is the basic healer. For several years before 1977 the CMC conducted a number of seminars and community meetings from which came a series of theological reflections upon the nature of the churches' ministry. These began to make an impact upon the way the churches expressed their concern for health.

Churches in rich countries were urged to rethink their health ministries at home as well as overseas. These discussions were undertaken against a backdrop of stunning statistics from surveys and information supplied by people on the frontlines. At least one million human lives are lost every year as a result of tetanus, a completely preventable disease. One hundred thousand children go blind each year from lack of vitamin A. Malaria remains the major health problem in tropical countries where an estimated 340 million live with endemic malaria. Up to 25 million children under five die each year in the developing world, one-third from diarrhoea from polluted water, one-quarter by respiratory diseases. Much of this occurs in rural areas where health expenditures are often four or five times less than in urban areas and where, in some countries, less than 15 per cent of the people have access to medical care.

The result of the theological reflections was an affirmation of a new understanding of "health, healing and wholeness", as CMC calls it. The Cyprus meeting of the CMC in 1980 produced a definition of health — "a dynamic state of wellbeing of the individual and the society — of physical, mental, spiritual, economic, political and social wellbeing, of being in harmony with each other, with the natural environment and with God".

Health here is understood not merely as freedom from disease, but wholeness. It points to a dynamic understanding of the harmony and completeness which health implies. And it helps identify the forces that work against health, calls for more shared responsibility for promoting our own and others' health, and offers the chance for congregations to become true healing communities. Many will understand it to say that social injustices in all their forms are barriers to wholeness.

Since 1979 the CMC has been involved in regional meetings to discuss the implications of this understanding of health. The titles describe the procedure: the Central American conference in Honduras in 1979 was on "The Churches' Role in Health and Wholeness" and the 1980 Southern Asia regional consultation in India was on "The Christian Understanding of Health, Healing and Wholeness". Other meetings have taken place in Bali for Southeast Asia, the Caribbean, the South Pacific and Africa.

The CMC staff has called the study which continues until 1983 an "exciting process with a fantastic mix of people. We have brought together professionals — from surgeons to midwives, administrators to nurses, pastors to social workers — evangelicals, Roman Catholics and Protestants, faith healers, Muslims and Hindus."

CMC is in no way a donor agency. It does not recruit or place personnel. Its funds go for the meetings that explore the issues of health and wholeness and occasionally to a small pilot project. The staff includes only four professionals, with administrative support. But even so, the staff does other consultative work with churches, with a strong emphasis on *primary health care*. The CMC pays tribute for what it has learned to those who are involved in the field, with their own theology and skills, in providing health care. "Our data base comes from this incredible constituency and we simply perform the synthetical function."

The World Health Organization, with which CMC has had close ties for many years (not least in the worldwide debate on the code of conduct for sales of infant formula) and a formal semi-annual conversation, has acknowledged the debt it owes to CMC for placing emphasis on primary health care and community-based concerns.

CMC has emphasized its concern for participation in the designing of primary care by those for whom the programmes are designed, the understanding that questions of justice, sustainability and equitable distribution are integral to the kind of development that makes wholeness possible. What makes people healthy, Kingma says, are meeting basic needs: food, water, housing, education, access to markets, roads, etc.

Other concerns. It has intensified its exploration of health issues as they relate to women. Attempts were made to raise consciousness about the disabled in its communications and field contacts, especially during the International Year of Disabled Persons, and other groups who also experience the "distant pity" of society: migrants, refugees, aged people, alcoholics, drug addicts, and other marginalized minorities.

CMC publishes *Contact* in four languages six times a year, a magazine with contributions from all over the world. Its circulation has reached 17,000 and is growing. One of its four languages is Portuguese, designed especially to reach Brazil and the African nations with Portuguese colonial histories for which so little literature is produced.

The work of CMC reveals a close relationship between the church's commitment to the poor and its ministry of healing. If the WCC has come to place a greater emphasis on a church in solidarity with the poor, its thinking has also been influenced by what the CMC has been learning in its work. Nowhere was this more clear than in the opening address by Philip Potter at the Central Committee meeting in Dresden in 1981. He used healing as a metaphor for the mission of the church:

> The essential nature of health is its source in God, i.e. beyond our own physical and social resources to the transcendent ground of our being. Medical and psychiatric research and practice are discovering more than ever that the real causes of illness are not just physical and social, but moral and spiritual, and that the healing process can only take place when the resources of the Spirit are mobilized for dealing with our ills.... The new perception of health as wholeness has opened up a new emphasis on harmony and reconciliation with the self, with other human beings and with God.

CHAPTER 5
THE GENERAL SECRETARIAT, STAFF AND FINANCES

General Secretariat

Last, certainly not least, but perhaps more specialized, come some words on the activities under the General Secretariat, the staff and on finances. Here are the support structures undergirding the efforts of the whole Council.

Philip Potter as General Secretary has the responsibility of seeing that the policies determined by the churches in the Assemblies and the Central and Executive Committees are carried out. It is a responsibility he shares with the three Deputy General Secretaries who are also the staff moderators of the three programme units. One practical way this occurs is through regular meetings of the staff executive group which includes the heads of all units.

Among the operations which relate directly to the General Secretariat is the *Ecumenical Institute* which for more than thirty years has offered ecumenical training for Christians from all over the world. Located at the lovely Chateau de Bossey, about twenty minutes and a world away from busy Geneva, it provides a course of study to about sixty students each year in a graduate programme running from October to February. It also has guest facilities in regular use by groups from all over the world, not least for various WCC meetings. Service there is supplemented by the famous "blue angels", volunteer young people from around the world.

Under the General Secretariat is the *Library of the Ecumenical Centre,* a unique collection of books and papers on the ecumenical movement, as well as the WCC's archives. It is an open library; hundreds of doctoral dissertations on ecumenical subjects owe their approval to the library's material.

The *Finance and Administration Department* includes the Office for Income Coordination and Development. Within it is the Assembly office, at work since 1980 getting ready for Vancouver. The personnel office and the documentation service are also located within administration.

110

The *Communication Department,* also part of the General Secretariat, has a variety of tasks, including issuing press releases, a weekly news service in English (Ecumenical Press Service), *Soepi* and *Mensuel* in French, *One World* (the monthly magazine), quarterly periodicals, books, radio interviews and a monthly tape service (Intervox). It does work with film and the visual arts and provides the language service. Much frustration accompanies the last task. The Council uses four operational languages — English, French, German and Spanish. Russian is added at large conferences. Obviously major third-world languages like Swahili and Chinese are missing and financial considerations are likely to keep this tension around for a long time. The department does much more than provide services. It sees itself as a resource for the whole Council in trying to overcome the communication gap that exists between its work and the potential recipients. In so doing, it has rejected a simple public relations approach in favour of a policy that tries to open the Council's work so that it can be seen as it is and speak for itself.

A New York office is located in the same building with the US National Council of Churches and is involved in interpretation of the WCC's work to member churches in the US.

Staff

Just before he left Geneva to return to his home country of India, Dr Stanley Samartha told his colleagues:

> I am grateful to the WCC for giving me the opportunity to serve the church through the ecumenical movement during these years. It has deepened my faith, extended my vision, and widened the horizon of my human concerns. Above all, it has enabled me to have so many friends not only among Christians — Protestants, Orthodox, and Roman Catholics in different countries — but also among neighbours of other faiths. During these years of shared concern and cooperative work, I have received far more than I was able to give. Without this enriching experience, my understanding of Jesus Christ "who suffered outside the gate" would have been far too narrow and my notion of God far too limited to sustain an extended Christian ministry.

The present staff working for the WCC come from about 45 countries and represent many more churches. When an executive position is open, member churches and councils, Central Committee and other committee members are informed. Names are submitted. In the personnel selection process, denominational and geographical balance is important.

Philip Potter is impressed by the many well-qualified people who are available to work for the WCC. "But the Council looks for that something extra, that combination of faith and involvement, the ability to contain within one person different cultures and different approaches, different ways of working, planning, handling meetings."

Not the least of the problems is the necessity of using English as the primary form of communication, both in spoken and written form. One staff person, responding to my comment about how articulate another staff member was about his work, said: "You ought to hear him in his own language; he is ten times more eloquent. He works here with a permanent limitation."

In the period since Nairobi the Council has applied a new rule for staff known as the nine-year rule. Executive staff are normally hired for three-year terms (the General Secretary and the three Deputy General Secretaries have five-year terms). Some people come for shorter periods for specified projects. The maximum extension is two further terms, making a total of nine years. In the past some outstanding individuals were retained for their whole careers. This Central Committee has acted firmly on the nine-year limit. Potter says that the rule "was created to remind us that the WCC exists as a traffic between the churches and not as a separate style of international civil service".

One staff change since the earlier days of the ecumenical movement which the nine-year rule is likely to encourage further seems to be the self-understanding of what the work of the Council and of the staff at heart really is. My own knowledge of the real nature of the days of the ecumenical pioneers may be too much conditioned by limited reading of their wide-ranging involvements. But I suspect the staff now see themselves much more working through the churches towards the ecumenical possibility than playing the role of leaders. A creative tension should be there, and is. But one could probably find in the staff considerable support for a statement made by Emilio Castro:

> The WCC is not a "superchurch", to do the task of the churches. We are only the servant of the churches, to help them support each other and inspire each other. The important thing is not what we do with our own programmes, but what the churches are doing all around the world. How can we help them help each other? In that modest role, there is a real ecumenical vocation.

The nine-year rule is sometimes bent — a few staff were extended to carry their work through the Vancouver Assembly in 1983 — but not now often broken. It means those who work in the ecumenical vortex know that they are returning to their churches to use their experience. It also assures fresh blood constantly flowing within the Council's bloodstream.

Yet it has difficulties. Some staff must depart with their work unfinished. It will shorten the ecumenical memory, the kind of perspective a Philip Potter brings into the current discussion. In some cases the political climate may make it impossible to return to home countries and finding any job at all may be difficult. When to bend the rules places a difficult human problem in the hands of the General Secretary and the Central Committee.

Finances

Good New Testament precedent exists for concern about money changers. For certain the WCC has paid a harsh penalty in recent years because it must engage in constant changing of money which comes to it in a wide variety of currencies. This is changed into Swiss francs to allow the Council to carry on its Geneva operations.

Perhaps only PCR has received more publicity in recent years than the financial difficulties experienced by the WCC. These have been real. They required staff reductions. They brought some programme limitations.

The primary explanation for the problem is simple. While the Swiss franc remained one of the world's most stable currencies, the US dollar, which many churches use to make their contributions, did not. Nor did many other currencies. In 1973 the exchange rate for the US dollar was Sfr.4.30. Thus a contribution of one million dollars was translated into Sfr.4.3 million. In 1977 the US dollar dropped to Sfr.1.48; the same one million dollar contribution now became Sfr. 1.48 million.

So, while in fact member churches were increasing their contributions to the Council's operating budget by as much as 50 per cent after Nairobi, the WCC had less money in Swiss currency to support its ongoing life and to carry out the tasks assigned by the churches. And the unpredictability of the exchange rate — from World War II until 1973 it was controlled, and therefore generally predictable — made budget projections a nightmare.

The good news is that these problems have affected primarily the central Geneva operations of the Council and not its worldwide service and interchurch aid projects which did not have to be converted into Swiss currency.

This is the important point. The problem was created by the wildly unpredictable foreign exchange market. The actual amount of money contributed to the general operating budget has increased substantially since Nairobi if calculated in "original currencies". In fact the money entrusted to the WCC to be used in other parts of the world has increased dramatically, from slightly over $17 million in 1970 to $33 million in 1978 to almost $70 million in 1980.

But the problem has been with the operating budget which covers programme and administrative costs for the Council's work.

Partly because of history, partly because of current trends, the Council receives both designated and undesignated income for its operating budget. Some of its sub-units have long-time relationships out of their history with agencies and churches which support them generously and directly. The contributions that come to the Council for their work are designated to be used by those sub-units and, often, for a particular project within that sub-unit.

But other parts of the Council do not have historical ties with any particular constituency. They are dependent upon funds received by the WCC as a whole, or perhaps from other sub-units when their work inter-relates. Six of the sub-units have been financially independent — CCPD, CWME, CICARWS, CMC, Office of Education and PTE. The rest of the Council's work depends primarily upon undesignated income. (Some "service departments", such as the Library, Finance, Personnel and Central Services, are largely financed by internal payments made for their services.)

So, the Council has a problem with foreign exchange. But it is also plagued by an imbalance between designated and undesignated income. Designated income can be used only as the donor and the Council agree. Undesignated income is available for any purpose and within any area of the Council. This in a real sense is the only income over which the WCC as an entity has full control.

In 1980 the operating budget of the WCC was about Sfr.30 million and only Sfr.4,968,781 was undesignated. By comparison, in 1973 Sfr.4,918,137 was undesignated. If inflation is accounted for, the Council had less money it controlled fully in 1980 than in 1973. (If the same amount of money in "original currencies" had been received and the US dollar-Swiss franc exchange rate had remained at the 1973 level, the Council would have at least twice as much undesignated money.) The only reason it had even this much in Swiss francs is that large donors, responding to pleas from the finance committee, increased their undesignated giving from 1976 to 1980 dramatically. For example, in original currency, undesignated giving from US churches went up 67 per cent, from the Netherlands by

33 per cent, from Sweden by 60 per cent, and from Canada by 93 per cent. The increases were wiped out by the exchange losses. That's called running hard to stay in the same place. In 1980 and 1981, however, with an improved exchange situation, the scene was brighter.

But still the tendency towards designated giving grows stronger, in spite of the response to this particular crisis. A number of reasons help to explain this development. Patrick Coïdan (France), Director for Income Coordination and Development, suggested several "simplified" reasons for a "complex reality".

Most of the undesignated giving originates in the central structures of the churches which themselves have been hit by inflation and show their own growing imbalance in what goes to central support and what to special appeals. "This is not just a WCC problem. We clearly reflect a problem of the churches."

Coïdan also points to the growing distrust of institutions, including the church; an emphasis by fund-raisers on specific projects for which funds are more easily available; the decline in membership in member churches in the North which have been traditionally supportive of the ecumenical movement; the decline in income in those churches where the funds flow upward as costs of maintaining local churches have risen dramatically (one recent study of US churches states that they are spending on the average 47 per cent more on fuel for heat than they did three years ago), making proportionately less money available centrally; the growing competition for funds from new religious organizations such as the electronic church (one US TV evangelist claims to receive $1 million a week to support his ministry).

It should be said here that, contrary to some expectations, the financial problems of the Council have nothing at all to do with the attacks it has undergone for its involvement in controversial issues. In fact, Coïdan refers to a paradox in funding. "We get support for what the churches criticize and we often don't get support for what they don't criticize. Everyone says Faith and Order should be at the heart of the work of the Council but it is not easy to find money for Faith and Order."

Potter says that "the churches have not used finances as a means to muzzle the Council. Once or twice this has happened but usually it is quickly made up from within those churches. The churches realize we cannot opt out of Christian obedience arising from what we have done and affirmed together."

But it does present two problems. One, some government agencies which want to be involved in projects that reach people at the base

115

believe the churches do a better job than governments. The Council has to decide how much government money it can distribute and on what terms it can accept such money.

Two, often the debate about WCC actions which draw fire takes place in the central structures of the churches — synods, judicatories — and in a few instances these bodies have cut funding to the WCC. Since that usually means a reduction in undesignated giving, the part of the WCC hurt by such cuts is in the largely non-controversial areas. At the same time other agencies of the same church may support the work that is being criticized. The problem is that the church does not deal with the issue itself; it avoids the internal debate by striking out at the WCC with one hand and supporting it with the other.

One church did deal with the problem internally. In the fall of 1981 the Swiss Protestant Church Federation heard from one of its member churches of its considerable displeasure with the WCC decision to withdraw its accounts from two major Swiss banks over their South African investments. After some debate, the Federation — which groups the Swiss reformed churches and is a member of the WCC — increased its contribution to the WCC for 1982.

Potter also believes that "the very controversial character of some actions has brought the churches much closer together".

The Church of England had to go through something of the same debate over the PCR grant to the Patriotic Front in Zimbabwe. Some funds were cut but the church sent a large delegation to Geneva for serious conversations, wrote a report about the work of the WCC, and the next year increased its contribution.

Beyond the designated and undesignated income which goes into the central operating budget, the third part of the budget involves those funds going to projects around the world which have shown such a rapid increase in recent years — from $17 million to $70 million in ten years. Obviously these too are designated funds. This money goes directly to the projects, with no WCC service charge, and no Swiss franc transaction.

The following figures (which represent percentages of the total WCC budget) suggest the pressures on undesignated giving when all three budget lines are listed:

	1978	1979	1980
Designated: projects	73%	80%	85%
Designated: budget linked	22%	16%	12%
Undesignated:	5%	4%	3%

One problem this identifies is that the dramatic increase in project funding flowing through the Council comes at a time when the staff has shown a decrease in numbers and the funds for the day-to-day operations of the Council have not kept up with inflation. The contributions by the churches and other agencies demonstrate a recognition of a willingness to participate ecumenically to meet undoubted needs. But something will have to give. The amount of funds that can be handled will have to be limited, the quality of administration will decline, or churches will have to provide more undesignated funds to support the central operation which makes possible the whole enterprise of sharing in this way.

Let it never be said that managing the finances of the WCC is an easy task. For several years, the budgets, trying to anticipate the exchange rate, still went out of kilter as the dollar-franc exchange rate dropped even faster. In recent years the Council tried to make budgeting for its sub-units simpler by establishing a guaranteed rate of exchange within the Council. But in the years since Nairobi the rate dropped faster than anticipated and the general fund had to make up the difference. In 1981 the dollar appreciated — it was about Sfr.2 per dollar at year's end — and the Council decided to support a month-by-month exchange rate within the Council. (But, still running hard to stay in the same place, inflation, which had been only about one per cent in 1977-1978, began to creep up to an average of just under four per cent in 1979-1980 and hit 6.5 per cent in 1981.)

The Executive Committee undertook a preliminary study in 1978 to consider possibly relocating the WCC headquarters to another city. Such a move would not be easy. It would require support of local member churches; freedom of speech, publication and press; ease of moving funds; access by individuals from member churches in all parts of the world; international communications; and a reasonably stable cost of living. Some comparisons were made. The costs of the move, a new building, and new equipment would be very high. Work would be disrupted. The Executive Committee reported to the Central Committee in 1979 that it did not "feel justified in authorizing a more detailed feasibility study and has agreed that the headquarters should remain in Geneva".

During this period discussions were also going on about the creation of an emergency reserve that would be Council-wide. Similar organizations maintain an emergency reserve in case of a cataclysm which would put the organization out of business or reduce its area of work substantially. For the WCC, the major costs would be severance pay for the staff and repatriating the non-Swiss staff. Some sub-units had their own emergency reserves. They agreed to place them into a common reserve but there was a problem. These funds were invested and the sub-units had budgeted the interest on them. The Central Committee decided to provide them with that interest for five years. After that, interest in the Council-wide reserve will be credited to the reserve to offset inflation.

Without question the discussions of specific financing have been placed against the backdrop of the growing conviction that the project form of sharing across national and regional lines is inadequate in an ecumenical fellowship. The discussion of ecumenical sharing of resources is one serious but uncertain attempt to move beyond donors and recipients into a solidarity that involves resources other than money.

ORGANIZATIONAL CHART OF THE WCC

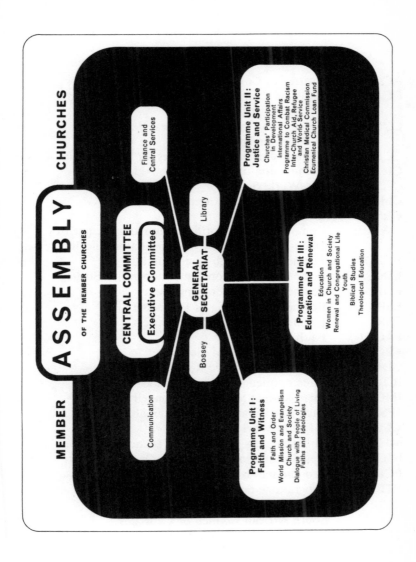

LIST OF ABBREVIATIONS

ACC:	Australian Council of Churches
CCA:	Christian Conference of Asia
CCC:	Chinese Christian Council
CCPD:	Commission on the Churches' Participation in Development
CCIA:	Commission of the Churches on International Affairs
CICARWS:	Commission on Inter-church Aid, Refugee and World Service
CMC:	Christian Medical Commission
C&S:	Church and Society
CWME:	Commission on World Mission and Evangelism
DFI:	Dialogue with People of other Faiths and Ideologies
ECLOF:	Ecumenical Church Loan Fund
EDCS:	Ecumenical Development Cooperative Society
EDF:	Ecumenical Development Fund
ESP:	Ecumenical Sharing of Personnel
ESR:	Ecumenical Sharing of Resources
F&O:	Faith and Order
FRG:	Federal Republic of Germany
GDR:	German Democratic Republic
ICBM:	Intercontinental Balistic Missile
IMC:	International Missionary Council
JPSS:	Just, Participatory and Sustainable Society
L&W:	Life and Work
MIT:	Massachusetts Institute of Technology
NIEO:	New International Economic Order
PCR:	Programme to Combat Racism
PTE:	Programme on Theological Education
RCL:	Renewal and Congregational Life
SACC:	South African Council of Churches
TEF:	Theological Education Fund
UIM:	Urban Industrial Mission
URM:	Urban Rural Mission
YWCA:	Young Women's Christian Association